Go Where the Fighting Was Fiercest

Go Where the Fighting Was Fiercest

The Guide to the Texas Civil War Monuments

Thomas E. Alexander and Dan K. Utley

State House Press

Buffalo Gap, Texas

Library of Congress Cataloging-in-Publication Data

Alexander, Thomas E.
Go Where the Fighting Was Fiercest: The Guide to the Texas Civil War Monuments
Thomas E. Alexander and Dan K. Utley
    p. cm.
Includes Bibliographical references and index.
ISBN-13 978-1-933337-57-9 (pbk. alk. paper)
ISBN-10 1-933337-57-5 (pbk. alk. paper)
1. History United States/Civil War Period (1850–1877) 2. Travel: United States / South West / West South Central (AR, GA, KY, LA, MS, NM, NC, PA, TX, VA) . 3. United States: History–19th century.
This paper meets the requirements of ANSI/NISO, Z39.48-1992 (permanence of paper)

Binding materials have been chosen for durability ∞
I. Title.
      "Cataloging-in-Publication Data available from the Library of Congress"

Manufactured in the United States
Copyright 2013, State House Press
All Rights Reserved
First Edition

State House Press
P.O. Box 818
Buffalo Gap, Texas 79508
325-572-3974 · 325-572-3991 (fax)
www.tfhcc.com

Printed in the United States of America
Distributed by Texas A&M University Press Consortium
800-826-8911
www.tamupress.com

ISBN-13: 978-1-933337-57-9
ISBN-10: 1-933337-56-5

Book Design by Rosenbohm Graphic Design

This book is a tribute to two groups who first set in motion the
commemorative efforts noted herein:
heritage tourists, who sought out the sites where history happened,
and members of the Texas Civil War Centennial Commission,
who worked selflessly to ensure there were monuments
in place to tell the stories of those who participated in the conflict.
With great appreciation, we dedicate this guide to them
and to their successors who understand that
history lives where history is told.

Publication supported in part by a gift
from John Nau, Houston, Texas.

Contents

Foreword: Theirs to Maintain

During the hottest days of summer 1861, Richmond, Virginia, was a hive of activity and promise. The fledgling Confederacy remained more concept than country, but the mood was pregnant with portents that a final Southern victory was certain—*and soon*. The constant arrival of enthusiastic and war-ready young men into the capital from the far corners of the would-be nation fed this conviction, and each arriving train brought evidence that independence would come. One trainload in particular carried with it a cargo of confidence. Piling out of the cars, these hotspurs assembled their ranks with a swagger born of distance—and history. They were Texans.

Days later these soldiers received their accouterments of war, their regimental flag, and the praise of Confederate officials. On this occasion, the president of the upstart republic came to welcome them to the cause. "The troops of other states have their reputations to gain," Jefferson Davis declared to these Lone Star reinforcements. "The sons of the defenders of the Alamo have theirs to maintain!"[1] With this simple appeal to the muse of history and the ego of youth, the most important man in the Confederacy set a high bar for fighters from west of the Sabine and south of the Red. In the months and years ahead, they did not disappoint.

Today, pink granite obelisks stand sentinel from far West Texas to Pennsylvania, marking the spots where these men defended their reputation and that of their state with sweat and blood, grit and faith. Because of their sacrifice and service, these sites are forever Texas, though often a long way from its borders. Grateful citizens made sure that future generations would remember their efforts; they continue this tradition as circumstances permit by placing additional markers wherever Texans held the line.

This book is a guide—and a reminder—of what Texas and Texans did in the US Civil War. Simultaneously practical and inspirational, *Go Where the Fighting Was Fiercest* provides historical context and physical settings for each of these monuments and serves as an excellent guide and introduction to the Civil War battlefields where Texans made—and maintained—their reputations as the best soldiers in the Confederacy.

Donald S. Frazier, Ph.D.
McMurry University, Abilene, Texas

---

[1] David G. McComb, *Texas, A Modern History*, revised edition (Austin: University of Texas Press, 2010), 71; Harold B. Simpson, Hood's *Texas Brigade* (Waco: Texian Press, 1970); 53; Mrs. Angelina Virginia Walton Winker, *The Confederate Capital and Hood's Texas Brigade* (Austin: Eugene Von Boeckmann, 1894), 33.

Preface

In 1995, the Texas Legislature approved the creation of a Military Sites Program within the Texas Historical Commission (THC) to record, preserve, commemorate, and interpret the stories and sites where Texas forces fought, both in and out of the state. Soon after, under the direction of THC Chairman John L. Nau, III, the agency undertook an extensive multistate survey of the Texas Civil War Monuments. The purpose of the survey was threefold: to assess the condition of the existing monuments placed in the 1960s by the Texas Civil War Centennial Commission; to facilitate restoration plans for those monuments in need of repair, utilizing local partnerships for both funding and maintenance; and to identify key battle sites where additional monuments might be placed, with funding from private sources.

In 1997, the THC inspection team of Stan Graves and Dan Utley—sometimes joined by John Nau and others—began visiting the various sites, from Anthony in far West Texas to Gettysburg in Pennsylvania. At each one, the team met with local or National Park Service (NPS) officials to determine specific preservation needs and to set appropriate timetables for the work. It was at the Kennesaw Mountain National Battlefield Park outside Atlanta that a park historian told the survey team that tourists from Texas were among the largest groups of park visitors outside the immediate area, and when they visited they always wanted to know how they could find the key positions where Texas forces fought. As the historian noted, "I usually tell them, go to where the fighting was fiercest, and there you'll find the Texas monument."

It is in honor of that spirit that we have embarked on this guidebook to long-ago scenes of fierce fighting, where forces on both sides of the conflict gave their best in support of both individual and collective causes. The reasons they fought may be found in other works; the purpose here is to commemorate site-based history that allows the current generation of historians and heritage tourists to walk the grounds of the battlefield and to determine their own sense of the past. History lives where history is remembered, and it is that guiding principle that forms the basis for this book.

The format of this book focuses on the nineteen military sites commemorated and interpreted in the Civil War Monuments Program, initiated by the State of Texas in the 1960s and continuing in operation today. Grouped in chronological order according to the date of battle, the sites are explored contextually by means of the setting, the battle, and the Texans who fought there. Then, additionally, in a unique presentation we believe brings the story to the present, we provide background on the history of the separate monuments, some of which have been central to their own subsequent battles over relevance or interpretation. We also reflect back to the Texas landscape of memory to provide information on how the state has remembered the battles and its own participants in the years since the Civil War through historical markers, county names, additional monuments, and other means.

Throughout the narrative the reader will also find brief sidebars of information that add dimension to the overall story. And finally, we conclude each battle description with an abbreviated list of suggested readings for those who would like to know more.

This, then, is a story of a past conflict, one that threatened to tear apart the foundations of the country's relatively brief existence. It is also, though, a story of commemoration—of how a group of people come together, regardless of their personal histories, to remember the past so its complexities might be better understood or contextualized. Equally important, however, is that this is a successful preservation story, one that continues through a unique partnership of public and private sources. There are still stories to be told and shared with the traveling public, and so the program continues more than forty years after it first began. Battlefield preservation, site interpretation, and cultural landscapes may have changed dramatically through the years, but the stories are still there, and there are still generations who need that information to guide their own set of values and historical comprehension. We hope the broad-based approach we offer here will add new dimensions to that never-ending exploration and perhaps to encourage open dialogue of the past.

Acknowledgments

This book could not have been possible without the generous and enthusiastic support of two men: John L. Nau, III of Houston and William A. McWhorter of Austin, both keen students of Texas history. These gentlemen, working in partnership, have endeavored to bring the intricate stories of the past to new audiences through recent battlefield interpretation. In so doing they have built on previous state efforts that date to the 1960s, when many of the sites noted herein were still the subject of planning debates over how best to mark and record the places where history happened. Thanks is also due to one of the unsung heroes of the Texas monument program, the late Austin businessman Jim Stasswender, who through his family business fabricated and personally placed many of the distinctive pink granite monoliths that grace historic sites in key battlefields across the United States.

Special thanks go to Donald S. Frazier, Ph.D., and Amy E. Smith of State House Press/ McWhiney Foundation Press. Quickly trusting in the validity of a concept, they set us on the right course from the beginning and were always ready to answer questions, provide encouragement, and offer suggestions as they kept us focused on the end product. They set a high standard for writer–editor teamwork, and we have greatly enjoyed working with them.

And no acknowledgments would be complete—or tolerated—without mention of our loving and supportive wives: Capy Alexander and Debby Davis Utley. Both have probably visited more battlefields than they bargained for, but they have always been there to encourage our interests in exploring history, wherever that might take us.

Thomas E. Alexander, Kerrville
Dan K. Utley, Pflugerville

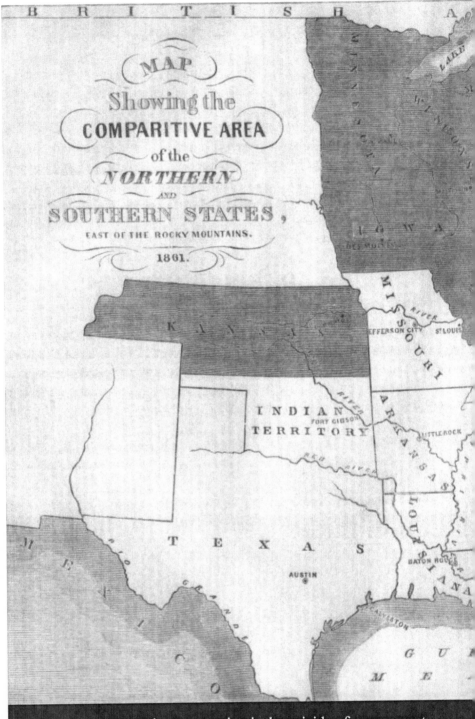

MAP

Showing the
COMPARITIVE AREA
of the
NORTHERN
AND
SOUTHERN STATES,
EAST OF THE ROCKY MOUNTAINS.
1861.

A surrender to secession is the suicide of government.
–*Cincinnati Commercial*

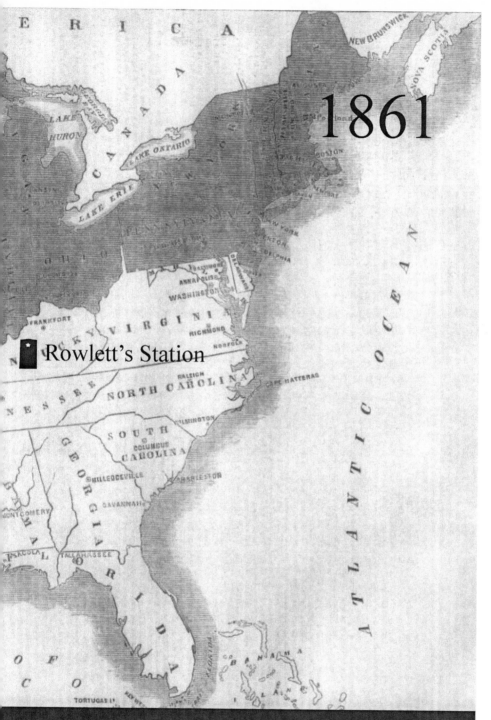

1861

Rowlett's Station

The Union is broken forever and the independence of the
South virtually established. –*London Times*

TEXAS

REMEMBERS THE VALOR AND DEVOTION OF
ITS SONS WHO SERVED WITH DISTINCTION ON
KENTUCKY BATTLEFIELDS DURING THE CIVIL WAR.

AT HOUSTON, TEXAS, DURING AUGUST AND SEPTEMBER 1861,
BENJAMIN FRANKLIN TERRY AND THOMAS S. LUBBOCK
ORGANIZED A CAVALRY REGIMENT THAT BECAME
THE CELEBRATED EIGHTH TEXAS. LED BY TERRY,
A RUSSELLVILLE, KENTUCKY NATIVE WHO WAS A
TEXAS PLANTER AND A MEMBER OF THE STATE
SECESSION CONVENTION, THE UNIT WAS KNOWN AS
TERRY'S TEXAS RANGERS. ON DECEMBER 17, 1861,
THE RANGERS—A CHARGING REGIMENT—ENGAGED
UNION TROOPS OF THE 32ND INDIANA VOLUNTEER
INFANTRY UNDER COL. AUGUST WILLICH IN THE
BATTLE OF ROWLETT'S STATION (WOODSONVILLE).
THE MILITARY OBJECTIVE WAS CONTROL OF THE
LOUISVILLE & NASHVILLE RAIL LINE, A VITAL SUPPLY
ROUTE THAT CROSSED THE GREEN RIVER NEARBY.
IN THE INITIAL CHARGE BY THE RANGERS, COL. TERRY
FELL, MORTALLY WOUNDED, AT THIS SITE. THE
OUTCOME OF THE BATTLE WAS INDECISIVE, BUT IT
PRESAGED EXPANSION OF THE WAR IN THE REGION
AND IS SIGNIFICANT FOR THE LOSS OF ONE OF TEXAS'
MOST BELOVED AND PROMISING FIELD LEADERS.

TERRY'S TEXAS RANGERS CONTINUED TO FIGHT ON
WITH DISTINCTION AT SHILOH, MURFREESBORO,
CHICKAMAUGA, PERRYVILLE, CHATTANOOGA,
ATLANTA AND BENTONVILLE, NEVER FORMALLY
SURRENDERING AS A UNIT. ITS SKILLS AS A LEADING
CAVALRY UNIT OF THE WESTERN THEATER AND ITS
WELL-DESERVED REPUTATION FOR BRAVERY AND
THE WILLINGNESS TO FIGHT DESPITE THE ODDS
HAD THEIR GENESIS IN KENTUCKY.

ERECTED BY THE STATE OF TEXAS 2007

Battle of Rowlett's Station, Kentucky

Also known as Battle of Woodsonville or Battle of Green River

December 17, 1861

The Situation

Although Kentucky was legally a slave state, it did not secede from the Union either before or during the Civil War. In May 1861, the legislature voted to remain neutral even though the state had strong economic ties to the South. In return, US President Abraham Lincoln, a native son of the Bluegrass State, pledged that Union forces would not cross Kentucky's boundaries as long as it was able to remain neutral. The state was almost equally divided in support of either the Union or the Confederacy. Men wishing to volunteer to serve in the opposing armies were free to do so. During the war, however, more than seventy-five thousand fought for the Union, whereas less than twenty-five thousand joined the Confederate Army. Nearly one-third of all Kentuckians who were in the war died while in the service.

> The Battle of Rowlett's Station took place less than thirty miles from the boyhood home of US President Abraham Lincoln and seventy-five miles from the birthplace of Col. Benjamin Franklin Terry.

The state's strategic geographical location was simply too important to sustain its highly desired neutrality. The presence of four significant rivers—Cumberland, Tennessee, Ohio, and most important, Mississippi—made Kentucky a key element in the military planning of both the Union and the Confederacy. For the North, the navigable waterways offered convenient access into the heart of the Confederacy. Fully

3

aware of this obvious geographical fact, the South was determined to block the enemy's use of the rivers.

In addition to the important access provided by the waterways, Kentucky was historically a vital overland passageway, which led from the more highly developed eastern United States to the beckoning and still largely uninhabited lands in the west. The legendary Daniel Boone had first blazed the trail westward through the Cumberland Gap, and in 1861 it remained a key thoroughfare for military movements from deep in the Confederacy to the vast important region that lay beyond the mountains. Besides its vital rivers and key western trails, Kentucky also had a well-developed railway system at the beginning of the Civil War. It was clear to both sides that control of that system would greatly affect the flow of men and matériel as the war progressed.

Early in the war, both Confederate and Union troops massed along the state's borders waiting for one or the other to make the first move to shatter the uneasy neutrality. The Confederacy finally succumbed to temptation on September 3, 1861, when Maj. Gen. Leonidas Polk moved across the state line to occupy the city of Columbus on the Mississippi River. The Union then wasted little time in crossing the Ohio River from Illinois to take Paducah. In command was a recently promoted and still largely unknown brigadier general named Ulysses S. Grant. In his memoir, Grant makes note of the fact that Confederate forces had hoped to occupy the city first and were only ten to fifteen miles away from it when his forces arrived.

Its perhaps naively desired neutrality shattered in just a few days' time, Kentucky quickly became the scene of a series of then seemingly insignificant battles that proved, in the long run, to be far more important than initially believed.

The Battle

Three months after the Confederates began their invasion of Kentucky, it became clear that the Union, although likewise an invader, seemed to be gaining the upper hand in the contest. What was actually more of a hit-and-run skirmish than a pitched battle took place on December 10, 1861, when US Brig. Gen. Alexander McDowell McCook's 2nd Division of the Army of the Ohio launched an attack on Confederate positions near the rail line at Munfordville, located some forty miles northeast of Bowling Green in the central part of the state. In an effort to deny their enemy the use of the important Louisville and Nashville Railroad tracks located in the region, the Confederates destroyed a section of the railway bridge that spanned the Green River. A temporary pontoon bridge enabled federal troops to cross the river, protect the men repairing the rail bridge, and then advance toward the small nearby community of Rowlett's Station.

On December 17, two companies of the 32nd Indiana Volunteer Infantry came into contact with elements of the 8th Texas Cavalry (better known as Terry's Texas Rangers), the 7th Texas Cavalry, and the 1st Arkansas Battalion. In relatively light fighting, the Union forces under Col. August Willich withdrew to a stronger defensive position after the combined 7th and 8th Texas Cavalry units charged to halt the federal advance. When word came that Union reinforcements were on their way to the site of the battle, the Confederates also fell back, leaving behind ninety-one casualties.

Among their fallen were the commander and organizer of the 8th Texas Cavalry, Col. Benjamin Franklin Terry, killed while leading the initial charge of his Rangers. A native of Kentucky, the colonel had been a wealthy sugar planter, former builder of railroads, and dedicated secessionist from the Houston, Texas area. Along with two other local men, Terry volunteered his services to the Confederacy in June 1861, receiving an initial appointment as an aide to Maj. Gen. James Longstreet with the rank of colonel.

Some sources claim the engagement at Rowlett's Station was a Confederate victory, perhaps in view of the fact that the Union forces withdrew from the fight before their opponent did. Other sources contend that the result of the battle was indecisive. In the broader view, however, the Union managed to control the general area after the skirmish, and with the trestle across the Green River quickly repaired, the Louisville and Nashville Railroad was once again in full operation. Within a month's time, the Union gained at least partial control of a sizeable section of Kentucky with its vital riverports and overland trails still intact.

The Texans

Although one source indicates that both the 7th and 8th Texas cavalries participated in the Battle of Rowlett's Station, most records indicate the 8th was the sole Texas unit on the field on December 17, 1861. Its senior officers, other than the ill-fated Colonel Terry, included John A. Wharton and Thomas S. Lubbock, who assisted Terry in organizing the regiment in Houston late in the summer of 1861. Other field commanders were Gustave Cook, Samuel Christian, Marcus L. Evans, Stephen C. Ferrill, Thomas Harrison, William R. Jarman, Leander M. Rayburn, and John G. Walker.

Gen. Alexander McDowell McCook, commander of the Union's 2nd Division of the Army of the Ohio at the time of its participation in the Battle of Rowlett's Station, was brother or cousin to thirteen other McCooks who fought in the Civil War. In 1896, as a retired major general, he represented the United States at the coronation of Czar Nicholas II in Russia.

The Texas Monument

With assistance from the Battle for the Bridge Historic Preserve in Kentucky, the Texas Historical Commission (THC) formally dedicated the monument for the Battle of Rowlett's Station in 2007. It was the first monument completed under the Texas Civil War Monument Fund, established to provide public financial support for battlefield commemorations. In placing the granite marker, the THC selected a small parcel of property believed to be the site where Colonel Terry died on December 17. In his official report of the battle, Confederate Gen. William J. Hardee noted: "The conduct of the Rangers was marked by impetuous valor. In charging the enemy, Colonel Terry was killed in the moment of victory."

The Texas monument at Rowlett's Station, Munfordville, Kentucky, marks the site where Col. Benjamin F. Terry died. Visible in the background is the rail line that was a key landmark on the day of battle. *Photo by Dan K. Utley.*

The idea is that the Texas monument at Rowlett's Station will prove to be a major landmark in ongoing efforts to preserve and interpret the battlefield, much of which remains in private ownership. The Battle for the Bridge Historic Preserve, the Hart County Historical Society, and others continue to work to bring attention to a lesser-known military conflict of the Civil War, but one that resulted in the loss of one of Texas' most beloved field commanders. As testimony to the respect and admiration his men had for their fallen leader, they continued to fight under the name Terry's Texas Rangers for the duration of the war.

Texans Remember

The legacy of Colonel Terry and his celebrated 8th Texas Cavalry is commemorated at various places in Texas. An equestrian statue designed by the noted sculptor Pompeo Coppini and placed in 1907 as tribute to Terry's Texas Rangers is located on the Capitol grounds in Austin, southwest of the main entrance. Official Texas Historical Markers for Terry can be found at Sugar Land, Fort Bend County, which developed under his influence, and at Sandy Point Cemetery, near Rosharon in Brazoria County, the site of his first interment. There is also a marker for him in Terry County, which is named in his honor, and at his final resting place in Glenwood Cemetery, Houston.

Directions to Monument

As of this writing there is no highway signage for the Texas monument, which is approximately 1.5 miles south of Munfordville. It sits in an open hayfield several hundred yards west of US 31W (Dixie Highway). Access to the site is open, but extreme caution is urged when visiting the site. The closest parking is on unpaved pull-offs along the busy highway, and there are no designated paths to the monument.

Suggested Readings

Bailey, Anne J. *Texans in the Confederate Cavalry*. Abilene, TX: McWhiney Foundation Press, 1995.

Blackburn, J. K. P., L. B. Giles, and E. S. Dodd. *The Terry Texas Ranger Trilogy*. Austin: State House Press, 1996.

Cutrer, Thomas W. *Our Trust Is in the God of Battles: The Civil War Letters of Robert Franklin Bunting, Chaplain, Terry's Texas Rangers*. Knoxville: University of Tennessee Press, 2006.

Marshall, Bruce, "Terry's Texas Rangers," *Civil War: The Magazine of the Civil War Society*, 10: 4 (July–August 1992): 40–44.

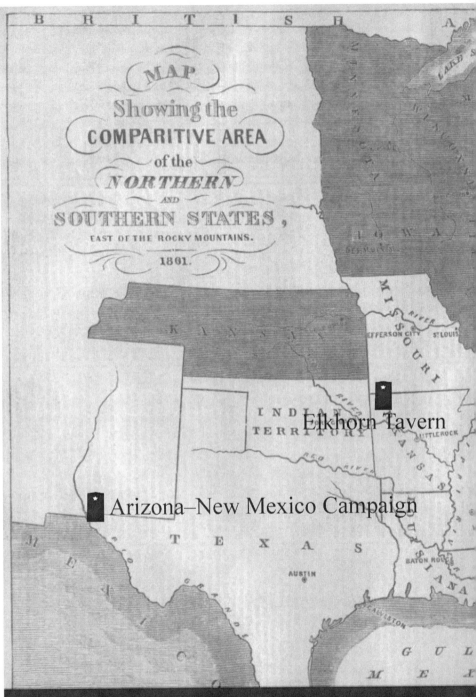

MAP Showing the COMPARITIVE AREA of the NORTHERN AND SOUTHERN STATES, EAST OF THE ROCKY MOUNTAINS. 1861.

Elkhorn Tavern

Arizona–New Mexico Campaign

I hope the day is not far distant when Genl. Sibley will be hung.
—*Texas veteran of Sibley's Brigade*

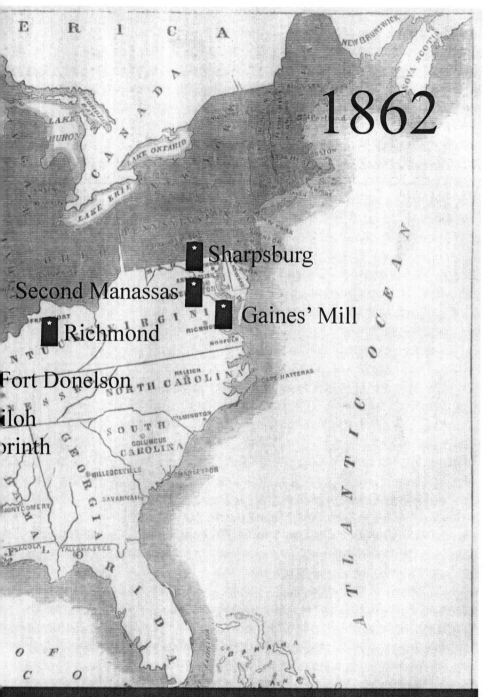

1862

Sharpsburg

Second Manassas

Gaines' Mill

Richmond

Fort Donelson

iloh

orinth

To secure the safety of the Mississippi River, I would slay millions.
n that point I am not only insane but mad. —*William Tecumseh Sherman*

TEXAS

REMEMBERS THE VALOR AND DEVOTION OF
HER SONS WHO SERVED AT FORT DONELSON
AND OTHER ENGAGEMENTS OF THIS THEATER
OF THE CIVIL WAR.

DURING THE BATTLE AT FORT DONELSON
FEB. 12-16, 1862 COL. JOHN GREGG'S
7TH TEXAS INFANTRY OF DAVIDSON'S
BRIGADE, JOHNSON'S DIVISION, WERE THE
RIGHT OF A GALLANT LINE WHICH DROVE
THE ENEMY FROM A HILL UNDER TERRIFIC
FIRE. IN SUPPORT OF CONFEDERATE GENERAL
WHEELER'S ATTACK ON THE FEDERAL GARRISON
AT FORT DONELSON, FEB. 3, 1863, *[sic]* THE
8TH TEXAS CAVALRY—TERRY'S TEXAS RANGERS—
OF WHARTON'S BRIGADE SET UP A ROAD BLOCK
8 MILES WEST OF DOVER AND SUCCESSFULLY
STOPPED THE UNION LAND REINFORCEMENTS
FROM REACHING THE BATTLE AREA. ALTHOUGH
COL. B.F. TERRY WAS KILLED AT THE BATTLE OF
WOODSONVILLE MORE THAN A YEAR BEFORE
THIS ACTION, THE RANGERS CONTINUED TO BE
KNOWN AS TERRY'S TEXAS RANGERS TO THE
WAR'S END. IN GEN. HARDEE'S SPECIAL
ORDERS IT WAS SAID OF TERRY: "HIS
REGIMENT DEPLORES THE LOSS OF A BRAVE
AND BELOVED COMMANDER; THE ARMY ONE OF
ITS ABLEST OFFICERS."

A MEMORIAL TO TEXANS
WHO SERVED THE CONFEDERACY

ERECTED BY THE STATE OF TEXAS 1964

Battle of Fort Donelson, Tennessee

February 12–16, 1862

The Situation

By mid-February 1862, it had become obvious to even the most optimistic of the Union's leaders that the Civil War was not going to be the successful brief encounter as initially believed. To the contrary, the ten months that had elapsed since the firing of the first shots of the war at Fort Sumter, South Carolina, proved to be deeply unsettling and sobering to Union commanders, as well as to the general populace of the United States. The embarrassing defeat of Union forces in the war's first major battle at Manassas, Virginia, on July 21, 1861, raised the previously unthinkable possibility of an ultimate Confederate victory in the war itself. This dire likelihood swept across the entire North and made imperative the need for an immediate and decisively strategic Union triumph on the field of battle.

The one individual most concerned about his army's inability to prevail over that of the presumably weaker new Confederate nation was US President Abraham Lincoln and, as such, commander-in chief of all those many Union soldiers who had broken ranks to flee in panic from the field at Manassas, just twenty-six miles from the White House in Washington, DC. Although Lincoln's actual military experience was limited to a brief stint as a captain of militia during the short Black Hawk War of 1832, he possessed an innate grasp of the overall strategic advantages the Union held by virtue of its overwhelming superiority in manpower, infrastructure, and industrial capability. He also possessed a master politician's sense of what his constituents demanded, coupled with the understanding of what he himself needed to do to be reelected in 1864. In short, Lincoln and his countrymen desperately needed a major victory in battle, and they wanted it immediately. Lincoln and his key advisors shared the view that any such significant victory should come about as part of a broad overall strategy centered on the concept of physically dividing the Confederate nation through a series of bold simultaneous strokes that would deprive it of the limited logistical assets that served to sustain it.

The first in the long and successful series of those early bold strokes took place at Fort Donelson, Tennessee, and its sister installation, Fort Henry, from February 12 to 16, 1862. As it developed, the campaign against the two forts also gave the Union its much desired truly significant victory in battle. The two Confederate forts were situated at key locations on the Tennessee and Cumberland rivers. Fort Henry on the Tennessee and Donelson on the Cumberland were some eleven miles apart on a narrow neck of land between the two rivers. They were on the Confederacy's line of defense that protected cities in Kentucky and western Tennessee. Although Kentucky was not a Confederate state, its largely pro-slavery stance made the placing of the river fortifications a seemingly prudent decision.

There were several factors that led to the Union plan to launch a campaign against the forts. From a strictly military point of view, their capitulation would clear the way into the very heart of the western part of the Confederacy. Politically, the fall of the forts would likely diminish the Confederacy's influence in Kentucky and help ensure that Missouri, another pivotal state that teetered on the brink of joining the newly formed Southern nation, would remain in the Union. Lincoln, devoted to restricting the growth of the Confederacy and preserving the Union at all costs in the process, placed a high priority on his army's river campaign in western Tennessee.

The Battle

The first phase of the federal campaign involved the use of gunboats to destroy Fort Henry before moving on to the more important Fort Donelson on the Cumberland River. The gunboats experienced little difficulty in obliterating their first objective, which was in fact already flooded by recent heavy rains that had fallen upriver. The Confederate soldiers from the ruined fort withdrew to travel the short distance overland to Fort Donelson. Their arrival swelled the size of the garrison there to more than twenty thousand troops. Situated on much higher ground and relatively safe from the flooding that contributed to the fall of its sister fort, Donelson was also heavily fortified and bristled with significant cannon. At first, the earthen fortification appeared to be strong enough to blunt and perhaps repel the attack of Union gunboats and ground troops. In this particular campaign, the various human factors at play arguably influenced the outcome of the battle more significantly than in any other Civil War battle.

The planner of the Fort Donelson campaign and also its field commander was the little-known Brig. Gen. Ulysses S. Grant. Thirty-

The full depth of the animosity and envy Maj. Gen. Henry W. Halleck held toward his onetime subordinate Brig. Gen. Ulysses S. Grant remained unknown by Grant until after the war. Following the victory at Fort Donelson, Halleck conspired to have Grant relieved of command and actually placed under arrest.

nine years of age at the time, Grant was a strong-willed and stubborn officer determined to rid himself of a beclouded service record that included a previous resignation on grounds of drunkenness on duty. In this, his first real opportunity to prove himself, Grant took on the dogged "victory at any cost" demeanor that would be his trademark throughout the rest of the war. His superior officer was Henry W. Halleck, an intellectual major general largely inexperienced in combat but exceptionally brilliant in writing about how to be successful in battle. Eager to change the army's perception of him as a scholar rather than a warrior, Halleck often sought credit for events even if it was not at all due. He also distrusted and disliked Grant, his subordinate, to the extent of spreading malicious untruths about him, particularly concerning his alleged drinking problem. Capitalizing on the opportunity of actually being on the battlefield directing the attack rather than languishing at his headquarters as Halleck had seen fit to do, it was Grant who made the Fort Donelson campaign a successful and decisive event, even though Halleck would claim credit for its outcome.

The leaders of the opposing force at the battle were every bit as contentious as their Union counterparts. The highly regarded Gen. Albert Sidney Johnston was overall commander in the Confederacy's vast Western Theater. For some curious and unknown reason, he had seen fit to post three brigadier generals to various command positions within Fort Donelson. The senior brigadier on the scene and the fort's commanding officer was John B. Floyd, a politician-turned-general with scarcely any military experience. His second in command was Gideon Pillow, an officer widely held in low regard throughout the army despite exemplary service in the Mexican War. The third general present at the river fort was Simon Bolivar Buckner, also a veteran of the Mexican War, but one with a good reputation among his fellow officers on both sides during the Civil War. He was not only a West Point classmate of General Grant but also a friend who had lent money to the very man whose Union forces were now moving toward the fort.

With this colorful if curious mix of opposing generals as a backdrop, the Battle of Fort Donelson commenced. Grant moved quickly to encircle the fort's earthworks overlooking the Cumberland. Perhaps much too occupied with the task of sorting out command responsibilities, the three Confederate generals failed to wholeheartedly attempt to thwart Grant's advance and encircling maneuver. Although previous attempts to level the besieged fortification by gunboat barrage failed, the arrival of reinforcements soon provided Grant with the necessary manpower to bring his attack force to twenty-seven thousand men, roughly six thousand more soldiers than were inside the fort.

When Grant briefly left the field to confer with the commander of the gunboat flotilla, the Confederates finally swung into action, venturing out of their works to gain a temporary advantage over their attackers. Reinforcements sent to the scene by General Johnston, however, proved to be inadequate to overcome the stranglehold Grant's forces had managed to establish. Once back on the field, General Grant prodded his men forward and soon attained a final position of superiority.

Generals Floyd and Pillow, having failed to take advantage of an excellent opportunity to escape Grant's clutches and still keep most of their command intact, decided instead to slink away by boat under cover of darkness, accompanied by fewer than 10 percent of their original force. With the exception of a large cavalry division led to safety by the rough-hewn Nathan Bedford Forrest, the balance of the defenders were left to fend for themselves as the Union noose tightened around the fort. In all, fifteen thousand Confederates became prisoners when Grant's men finally swept over the earthworks. Union losses were nearly three thousand killed or wounded.

It fell to Brigadier General Buckner, the only Confederate general still remaining at the fort, to offer a formal surrender to Grant, his friend and classmate. Although he bristled at Grant's insistence that the surrender be unconditional, Buckner did meet with the Union commander in what reportedly was a convivial reunion that gave General Grant his first significant victory of the Civil War. On the greater national stage, it also was the major battlefield victory that Lincoln so sorely needed.

As a result of the victory at Fort Donelson, the road to the core of the Confederacy opened to Union military action. Although General Halleck claimed the victory as being of his doing, Lincoln and the entire North knew the name of the true hero of the river campaign. From that time onward, he would be popularly known as "Unconditional Surrender" Grant.

Union forces captured Brig. Gen. Bushrod Rust Johnson, in whose division the Texas 7th Infantry Regiment served at Fort Donelson, when the fortification fell to General Ulysses S. Grant. Johnson managed to escape, however, and fought on throughout the rest of the war. As a major general, he was paroled at Appomattox Court House, Virginia, in 1865, along with many other Confederate general officers.

As Grant and his victory were celebrated throughout the North, the Confederacy's army in the West began moving back to the East. It had suffered its first major defeat of the war, and Lincoln's divide-and-conquer strategy had been placed irreversibly in motion. In a sense, the Battle of Fort Donelson, though early in a war that would rage on for years, laid the foundation for the ultimate end of the Confederacy. Lincoln had found his general, and that officer, increasingly relentless, would drive on to crush the rebellion in 1865.

The Texans

The best known Texas leader involved in the Fort Donelson battle was Confederate General Albert Sidney Johnston, commander of all Southern armies in the West. Although his decision to only marginally reinforce the besieged fort, coupled with his failure to come personally to the battlefield to take full command, generated criticism throughout the South, Confederate President Jefferson Davis continued to view him as the "finest general on either side during the Civil War." The only Texas unit that saw service at Fort Donelson was the 7th Texas Infantry Regiment, part of Davidson's Brigade, Johnson's Division.

The Monument

Recreational and residential development has encroached on remaining elements of the Fort Donelson battlefield, and modern changes in the cultural landscape are evident in the area near the Texas monument. Located in the vicinity of the historic Forge Road southeast of the fort and south of the town of Dover, Tennessee, the monument interprets the Texans' role in an early morning attack on February 15 by Confederate forces in an attempt to open an escape route through the Union right flank. After fierce fighting that covered considerable ground, the Confederates pulled back to their line of entrenchment, and Union forces eventually sealed the breach. Many of the earthworks that were at the center of the fighting, including an extensive line immediately to the east of the Texas position, have been lost through time.

Col. John Gregg led the 7th Texas Infantry as part of a bold sweeping action under intense enemy fire that initially drove Union forces from the area around Fort Donelson, but the gain proved to be of short duration. *Courtesy of Library of Congress, LC-USZ62-134003.*

Texans Remember

Texas participants in the fighting at Fort Donelson who are commemorated with Official Texas Historical Markers include:

- Stockton P. Donley (1821–1871), a native of Kentucky and a captain in the 7th Texas Infantry, who served briefly as a Texas Supreme Court Justice after the war. Donley County in the Texas Panhandle is named in his honor, and a monument to him is located in the county seat of Clarendon.
- Mississippian Hiram B. Granbury (1831–1864), organizer of the Waco Guards at the onset of the Civil War, was a major in the 7th Texas Infantry at Fort Donelson. Captured at Donelson and released at Vicksburg, he fought on for the South and was one of six Confederate generals killed in the battle of Franklin, Tennessee. The town of Granbury, county seat of Hood County in North Central Texas, is named in his honor.
- John Gregg (1828–1864), organizer and colonel of the 7th Texas Infantry, rejoined the Confederate Army following his capture at Fort Donelson and was severely wounded at Chickamauga. He died in fighting near Richmond, Virginia, in 1864. Gregg County, in East Texas, is named for him, and a monument to

This photo from the 1990s shows a National Park Service (NPS) employee touching up the wording on the Texas monument at Fort Donelson. A joint preservation partnership between the Texas Historical Commission and the NPS provided for the refurbishing of the monument texts, which had become illegible over time. *Courtesy Texas Historical Commission.*

his distinguished career in government and military service is located on the courthouse square in the county seat of Longview.

- William L. Moody (1828–1920), born in Virginia, organized Company G of the 7th Texas Infantry out of Freestone County. Captured at Fort Donelson, he eventually returned to Texas and later became a leading citizen of Galveston, where his family proved particularly influential in the town's dramatic commercial development through the years.

- Khleber Miller Van Zandt (1836–1930), of Tennessee, raised Company D of the infantry. Captured at Fort Donelson but later exchanged at Vicksburg, he continued fighting for the Confederacy and served in such key battles as Atlanta, Franklin, and Chickamauga, where he became the unit leader following the wounding of Granbury. After the war, Van Zandt moved to Fort Worth, where he became a prominent merchant, newspaperman, landowner, and railroad promoter, serving for a brief time as a state legislator.

Directions to Monument

The monument is located south of Dover along Natcor Drive (CR 943), west of Main Street and east of Cedar Street. For more specific directions, check at the park visitor center, 120 Fort Donelson Road, Dover.

Suggested Readings

Cooling, B. Franklin. *Fort Donelson's Legacy: War and Society in Kentucky and Tennessee, 1862–1863*. Knoxville: University of Tennessee Press, 1997.

———. *Forts Henry and Donelson: The Key to the Confederate Heartland*. Knoxville: University of Tennessee Press, 1987.

Gott, Kendall D. *Where the South Lost the War: An Analysis of the Fort Henry-Fort Donelson Campaign, February 1862*. Mechanicsburg, PA: Stackpole Books, 2003.

Knight, James R. *The Battle of Fort Donelson: No Terms But Unconditional Surrender*. Charleston, SC: The History Press, 2011.

Tucker, Spencer. *Unconditional Surrender: The Capture of Forts Henry and Donelson*. Abilene, TX: McWhiney Foundation Press, 2001.

TEXAS
REMEMBERS THE VALOR AND DEVOTION OF
HER SONS WHO SERVED AT ELKHORN TAVERN
(PEA RIDGE, ARKANSAS)
MARCH 7-8, 1862.

IN VAN DORN'S ATTACK OF MARCH 7, THESE
TEXAS UNITS UNDER BRIG. GEN. BEN.
McCULLOCH ASSAULTED THE UNION HIGH
CENTER.
3RD TEXAS CAVALRY (SOUTH KANSAS-TEXAS
REGT.)—COL. ELKANAH GREER, LT. COL. WALTER
P. LANE.
CAPT. O.G. WELCH'S SQUADRON (ATTACHED TO
3RD TEXAS CAVALRY).
6TH TEXAS CAVALRY—COL. B.W. STONE.
YOUNG'S (11TH) TEXAS CAVALRY—LT. COL.
JAMES J. DIAMOND.
SIMS' (9TH) TEXAS CAVALRY—COL. WILLIAM
SIMS, LT. COL. WILLIAM QUAYLE.
WHITFIELD'S (4TH) TEXAS CAVALRY BN.—
MAJ. JOHN W. WHITFIELD.

TEXAS UNIT SUPPORTING MAJ. GEN
STERLING PRICE'S FLANK ATTACK ON THE
UNION EXTREME LEFT AND REAR WAS
GOOD'S BATTERY—CAPT. J.J. GOOD.

BRIG. GEN. BEN McCULLOCH OF TEXAS WAS
KILLED IN THE ACTION. "A BOLDER SOLDIER
NEVER DIED FOR HIS COUNTRY"—VAN DORN.

A MEMORIAL TO TEXANS
WHO SERVED THE CONFEDERACY

ERECTED BY THE STATE OF TEXAS 1964

Battle of Elkhorn Tavern, Arkansas

Also known as Battle of Pea Ridge

March 7–8, 1862

The Situation

The bloody struggle between the Union and the Confederacy for control of the state of Missouri began in June 1861, two months following the beginning of the Civil War. Following the Battle of Wilson's Creek on August 10, 1861, it appeared the Confederacy was poised to prevail in the struggle and that Missouri, a slave state, would likely secede from the Union. As the year 1861 came to a close, a renewed federal military effort was launched to drive the Confederates from the state and retain Missouri within the Union. US President Abraham Lincoln had, from the very first of the war, sensed that the control and retention of the state was critical to the Union cause. Despite previous losses, the president continued to put pressure on his army to redouble its thus far ineffective efforts to drive the Confederate forces from the state once and for all.

James Butler Hickok, who would later become known as the legendary frontiersman, "Wild Bill" Hickok, served as a scout for Brig. Gen. Samuel Ryan Curtis during the battle.

Early in 1862, a Union Army force of eleven thousand began a drive in Missouri to strike the Confederate forces commanded by Sterling Price, the general who had helped fashion the South's previous decisive victory at Wilson's Creek. Commanding the large Union Army was Brig. Gen. Samuel Ryan Curtis, a veteran of the Mexican War and a recently retired US congressman from Iowa.

Outnumbered, Price withdrew his command into Arkansas to join the colorful Brig. Gen. Ben McCulloch, his co-victor at Wilson's Creek. The two Confederate generals halted their combined commands at Fayetteville, roughly thirty miles south of the Missouri state line. General Curtis, in the meantime, had ordered his men into a strong defensive position at a place called Elkhorn Tavern, thirty miles north of Fayetteville.

On March 2, 1861, Maj. Gen. Earl Van Dorn, newly named commander of the Confederate's Army of the West, arrived at the Price–McCulloch encampment in the Arkansas mountains near Fayetteville. Also a veteran of the Mexican War, Van Dorn had later served with distinction on the Texas frontier during the peak of the Indian Wars. He was short in stature but long on daring and impatience. Moving up in rank from US Army major to Confederate major general in just nine months, the often overly zealous Van Dorn was eager to gain even more recognition and the higher rank that would likely accompany success in battle.

Wasting no time in his quest for glory, Van Dorn ordered Price and McCulloch to march back to Missouri just two days after he had arrived at their joint encampment. Joining the northward march were three regiments of Indians that had been recruited to the Confederate cause by Brig. Gen. Albert Pike in what is today the state of Oklahoma. Pike had been appointed to his rank directly from civilian life for the primary purpose of negotiating with the elders of the five Indian tribes to raise troops for the Confederacy.

Field commander of the Five Nation warriors was Col. Stand Watie, a three-quarter Cherokee. He had survived the infamous eviction of his tribe and the following forced march to the Indian Territory to become an influential leader of his tribe. Following the Confederate victory at Wilson's Creek, Watie organized a unit known as the Cherokee Mounted Rifles. He served the Confederacy with distinction during the entire war and was the last general to surrender to Union forces a month after the war ended.

Van Dorn's combined force of nearly seventeen thousand men marched northward back into Missouri despite a heavy springtime blizzard. General Curtis, learning of the Confederate advance, ordered his men into consolidated defensive positions just south of a brooding rocky precipice known as Pea Ridge, near Elkhorn Tavern. Curtis had more than ten thousand troops in place on March 6, the day of the battle.

The Battle

The first clash in the battle came as Van Dorn's advance guard overtook their enemy's rear guard, commanded by Brig. Gen. Franz Sigel. It was Sigel who had led his soldiers in an inglorious retreat during the Battle of Wilson's Creek and now, once again, the hapless Sigel retreated back to where General Curtis had established his line of defense.

When Van Dorn's two divisions, led by generals McCulloch and Price, reached the Union defenses, the usually aggressive senior overall commander reasoned that to attack frontally would be folly, even though he outnumbered Curtis by some seven thousand troops. Rather than risk reducing that numerical advantage, Van Dorn ordered his men to flank Curtis's defensive line to attack the Union force from the rear. To confuse his enemy, Van Dorn's men set many campfires that glowed throughout the cold dark night, convincing most of the Union men that morning would bring a direct attack launched by the Southern soldiers now presumably resting up for battle around those twinkling firesides.

General Curtis was among the few not deceived by Van Dorn's trickery. Once he discovered his wily opponent's intentions, Curtis swung his entire army to its rear to face north toward Pea Ridge, where Van Dorn's army poised to attack. Although the Union position now put their well-developed line of entrenchments behind them instead of providing a defense at their front, the determined Curtis chose to meet his foe head on.

Brig. Gen. Albert Pike, organizer of the Indian warriors who fought at Elkhorn Tavern, promised Maj. Gen. Earl Van Dorn that at least 7,000 warriors would be at the battle, but fewer than 2,300 actually came ready to fight. Some were accused of scalping dead and wounded Union soldiers in the field during the battle.

One Union division promptly met an enemy unit never before encountered in any conventional war setting. Pike's warriors from the Indian Territory, dressed in ceremonial battle regalia and commanded by Colonel Watie, struck fear in the hearts of the Union soldiers. Few of the men had served on the Texas frontier before the war and were thus totally unnerved by the screaming horde that raced toward them, brandishing tomahawks as well as muskets, seemingly oblivious to the potential destructive power of the Union artillery. When the power of those weapons finally made its impression, the Indians' thirst for this formal kind of white man's warfare quickly dissipated. Their attack had been for the most part more frightening than effective, and just as suddenly as they had rushed the Union line, the Indians seemingly melted away into the nearby brush after enjoying a brief celebratory war dance.

As the Indians disappeared, General McCulloch led his division in a fierce charge across an open field. Not known for wearing anything resembling a formal uniform, the colorfully attired Confederate leader was probably a more likely target than some suitably uniformed officer. At any rate, a sharpshooter's bullet ended the life of the general who had survived his encounters with Antonio López de Santa Anna's soldiers on the plains of Buena Vista fourteen years previously in Mexico only to die on a field in Arkansas.

News of McCulloch's death spread rapidly throughout his immediate command and well beyond. It seemed his men's will to continue fighting had died along with their beloved commanding general. When his second in command was killed soon after, the fighting in one sector of the battle came to an abrupt end.

The battle continued, though, at other points around Pea Ridge and Elkhorn Tavern, raging on until darkness fell. The next day, Van Dorn ordered his fatigued soldiers to advance directly toward the tavern. As a result of Van Dorn's inefficient staff coordination,

During the intense fighting around the Elkhorn Tavern along the Telegraph Road near Pea Ridge, Arkansas, owners Joseph and Lucinda Cox lived with their family in the basement. The original building later burned to the ground, but the owners rebuilt. Courtesy of Library of *Congress, HABS ARK, 4-PEARI.V,1--1.*

however, his men soon ran out of ammunition. The tide of battle then turned slowly in favor of the Union and Van Dorn could only retreat to the south.

The Confederates suffered casualties of more than two thousand, whereas the outnumbered Union force lost about two-thirds as many. As a reward for his victory, General Curtis received promotion to major general and shortly thereafter assumed command of the Union's Department of the Missouri. His principal opposing general in the battle never attained the higher rank he had so zealously and incautiously pursued at Pea Ridge. Van Dorn did, however, distinguish himself later in the war as a brilliant cavalry commander, only to be assassinated in his headquarters by an outraged and cuckolded husband in 1863.

As a result of its defeat at Elkhorn Tavern, the Confederacy would no longer claim Missouri as being totally theirs. The defeat also led directly to the Union invasion of Arkansas.

The Texans

Texas units involved in the Battle of Elkhorn Tavern were:
- 3rd Texas Cavalry (South Kansas–Texas Regiment, with Capt. O. G. Welch's Squadron attached)
- 6th Texas Cavalry Regiment
- Sims's 9th Texas Cavalry Regiment
- Whitefield's 4th Texas Cavalry Battalion
- Good's Battery

The Monument

In the files of the Texas Historical Commission (THC) are several pieces of correspondence from the 1960s dealing with the so-called "case of the misplaced marker" at Pea Ridge. For background, it is important to note the Texas monument is on the grounds of a local public school and not at the death site of McCulloch within the boundaries of the national park. The apparent exclusion came as the result of misunderstandings and miscommunication that developed between the State of Texas and the National Park Service (NPS). According to Frank LaRue (of Athens, Texas), who served on a special advisory board for the Texas State Historical Survey Committee (TSHSC), precursor of the THC, he first became aware of the placement issue on April 11, 1965, when he arrived at Pea Ridge to inspect the new monument in preparation for its dedication. There, he met with a delegation of local men comprised of the park superintendent, the mayor, and the chamber of commerce manager. Meeting at a coffee shop near the school and the new monument site, LaRue was first advised that the NPS could not accept the monument and that unless it could be given to the City of Pea Ridge, there would be no dedication. Unable to contact TSHSC officials by phone, and therefore acting without official authority, he agreed to the relocation, hoping the matter might be resolved more satisfactorily later.

The controversy allegedly stemmed from a decision by the park superintendent to limit the number of markers, monuments, and signs in the park. Such a decision likely had NPS backing at some level, but the superintendent may also have been particularly zealous in carrying out the plan. Regardless, the dedication ceremony went forward, and LaRue, representing the State of Texas, formally gifted the Texas monument to the City of Pea Ridge. What followed was a barrage of inquiries, public pleas, resolutions, Associated Press newspaper articles, and complaints that reached all the way to the president of the United States and the Department of the Interior. Perhaps as a result, the park superintendent soon received a new assignment, but the monument remained on the school grounds, where, LaRue later noted, it shared space with a chamber of commerce log cabin, as well as "a variety of road signs, a motel sign and a bank sign." LaRue was among the most vocal opponents of the school site, and when he failed to receive the type of support he felt he needed from the TSHSC, he pushed other options, including support from historical groups and the state legislature. What frustrated LaRue in particular was that the Pea Ridge

A recent photo of the Texas monument for the Battle of Elkhorn Tavern shows its location within the modern setting of the Pea Ridge Schools campus. *Courtesy of Texas Historical Commission; Joe Cavanaugh, photographer.*

monument was the last in the initial series of monuments sponsored by the state, so there were already well-established precedents for placing Texas monuments within both state and federal battleground parks.

Throughout 1965, supporters on both sides of the issue worked to rally their forces, and the correspondence reflects the intensity of the situation. Writing two days before Christmas in 1965, Mrs. W. W. Vaught, the Commander of the Third District of the Arkansas Civil War Centennial Commission, sent a letter to John Ben Shepperd, a commissioner of the TSHSC. Responding to Shepperd's previous statement that he was satisfied with the monument location, she wrote, "If you just wanted a place to put your Texas Monument honoring the Texas soldiers, why in this world didn't you set it somewhere in Texas? That would have done just as well and saved us the explaining here about why it is in the village of Pea Ridge seven miles from the battlefield." And then, ratcheting up the rhetoric, she added, "It seems to me very callous that men like you are not conscious of the disrespect this shows for our fighting men, especially now that so many are being sacrificed in the present disastrous war in Viet Nam." Only a few days into the new year, Shepperd sent a copy of the letter, along with other correspondence, to Truett Latimer, then executive director of the TSHSC, stating, "As far as I am concerned, this closes the matter out. . . ."

Despite the efforts of state leaders to end the controversy, it continued to smolder for awhile. Among those who took up the cause was James E. Murray of Rogers, Arkansas, who described himself as "An Interested Civil War Buff Who Would Like to Know What Happened, When and Where." Serving as the local watchdog on the matter, he frequently wrote to Texas officials, noting in one letter that the NPS staff had subsequently altered its "no monument" stand, but that "Since the change in policy, the National Park Service has been unable to get the monument moved to its intended place, the park. This is rather unusual because one of the employees of the Pea Ridge Park was elected to the City Council . . . and has two brothers-in-law on the council of four. Yet, the Park Service is unable to straighten out the error."

There evidently followed a series of unofficial inquiries regarding the monument matter, and in September 1967, Murray reported: "The city council met in a called session Monday evening and the monument subject was brought up. After considerable heated discussion one of the anti-monument faction presented a motion that the monument remain on the Pea Ridge school ground in Pea Ridge. . . . As of now as far as the council is concerned they are not in favor of the monument being moved. This present skirmish we lost but we haven't lost the war."

According to Murray and others at the time, the location of the Texas monument on the school grounds was a temporary solution to the larger issue of monumentation within Pea Ridge Battleground National Park. Although some saw it as an effort to hold the monument in public trust until a viable solution could be brokered, it nevertheless formally transferred to the City of Pea Ridge, albeit without proper authority. So, despite a number of unofficial contacts through the years and the confusion of countless heritage tourists, the Texas monument remains on the school grounds, where it interprets a story that developed several miles away.

Texans Remember

Among the various Official Texas Historical Markers referencing the Battle of Elkhorn Tavern (Pea Ridge) are two for General McCulloch: one at Brady, in McCulloch County, named in his honor; and the other at the site of Camp Ben McCulloch near Driftwood, Hays County, where former Confederates and their families met in 1896 to organize the Camp Ben McCulloch Chapter of the United Confederate Veterans. There are also markers for participants of the fighting at Pea Ridge, including: Elkanah Greer (courthouse grounds, Marshall, Harrison County), who raised the 3rd Texas Cavalry; Illinois native Alfred M. Hightower (6600 Smithfield Road, North Richland Hills, Tarrant County), a mounted rifleman in the battle and later a rancher in Kansas; Virginia native and West Point graduate William L. Cabell (Greenwood Cemetery, Dallas), who became a brigadier general

> The bodies of both Brig. Gen. Ben McCulloch and his second in command, Brig. Gen. James McIntosh, slain within minutes of each other at Elkhorn Tavern, are buried in the Texas State Cemetery in Austin.

after Pea Ridge and, following the war, moved to Texas and served as mayor of Dallas for several terms; John W. Whitfield (Memorial Park, Hallettsville, Lavaca County), who formed Whitfield's Legion that served with distinction in Mississippi; and H. P. Mabry (2900 Crestline

Road, Fort Worth), a Georgia native who became a Texas legislator prior to military service in Indian Territory, Missouri, Arkansas, and Mississippi, and who later practiced law in Fort Worth. There are also state markers in Sherman, Grayson County, for the 9th Texas Cavalry and 11th Texas Cavalry (100 W. Houston St.).

Directions to the Monument

Northeast corner of the intersection of Pickens Road (Arkansas 72) and N. Curtis Avenue (Arkansas 94), Pea Ridge.

Suggested Readings

McKnight, James R. *The Battle of Pea Ridge: The Civil War Fight for the Ozarks.* Charleston, SC: The History Press, 2012.

Shea, William L. *War in the West: Pea Ridge and Prairie Grove.* Abilene, TX: McWhiney Foundation Press, 2001.

Shea, William L., and Earl J. Hess. *Pea Ridge: Civil War Campaign in the West.* Chapel Hill: University of North Carolina Press, 1997.

TEXAS

REMEMBERS THE VALOR AND DEVOTION OF
HER SONS WHO SERVED IN THE ARIZONA-NEW
MEXICO CAMPAIGN OF 1861-62.

SIBLEY'S AND BAYLOR'S TEXAS TROOPS
FOLLOWED THIS ROUTE IN THE EXPEDITION
TO OCCUPY AND HOLD THE TERRITORY OF
NEW MEXICO (PRESENT DAY ARIZONA, NEW
MEXICO AND PART OF NEVADA) AND TO
EXTEND THE CONFEDERACY TO THE PACIFIC.
BAYLOR PROCLAIMED PROVISIONAL
GOVERNMENT FOR TERRITORY OF ARIZONA,
ASSUMED GOVERNORSHIP; SIBLEY TOOK
MILITARY COMMAND. ONE SKIRMISH WITH
UNION FORCES TOOK PLACE FORTY MILES
WEST OF TUCSON, ARIZONA AND SOUTHERN
SCOUTS VENTURED WITHIN EIGHTY MILES OF
CALIFORNIA. THE CONFEDERATES WON THE
HARD FOUGHT BATTLE OF VAL VERDE FEB.
21, 1862, TOOK ALBUQUERQUE AND SANTA FE
AND WENT ON TO VICTORY AT BATTLE OF
GLORIETA MAR. 28, 1862. THE DISCOVERY AND
DESTRUCTION OF SIBLEY'S SUPPLY TRAIN
BY A UNION FLANKING FORCE LEFT THE
TEXANS WITHOUT MILITARY SUPPLIES AND
SUBSISTENCE AND WITHDRAWAL OF THE
EXPEDITION BECAME NECESSARY.
AS GETTYSBURG MARKED THE "HIGH TIDE"
OF CONFEDERATE PENETRATION TO THE
NORTH, SO GLORIETA MARKED THE CLIMAX
OF CONFEDERATE EXPANSION TO THE WEST.

A MEMORIAL TO THE TEXANS WHO SERVED THE CONFEDERACY

ERECTED BY THE STATE OF TEXAS 1963

Arizona–New Mexico Campaign, Texas

Monument originally slated for Glorieta Pass, New Mexico

1861–1862

The Situation

Given that it held the rich if rare promise of offering much to gain with very little to lose, the Confederacy's plan to launch a military campaign in far off New Mexico Territory seemed on its surface to be exceptionally sound. Having just resigned his commission as a major in the US army when the Civil War commenced, Henry Hopkins Sibley left his post as the commander of Fort Union, New Mexico Territory, to travel as swiftly as possible to the Confederate capital at Richmond, Virginia. His mission was to present his bold strategic plan to his longtime friend, and now his commander-in-chief, President Jefferson Davis. The plan, which Sibley apparently concocted as he traveled eastward, was to launch a bold strike against the relatively weak Union military positions situated along the Rio Grande near El Paso, Texas, and then eventually to occupy Albuquerque and then the territorial capital of Santa Fe. Once all that had been accomplished, Sibley envisioned overpowering Fort Union, located some seventy-five miles northeast of Santa Fe. From there, the Confederate forces could move swiftly up into Colorado Territory with its rich fields of gold and silver.

Thus enriched, Sibley reasoned, the Confederates would next easily extend their western invasion to occupy present-day Arizona, Nevada, and in time, California, with its own treasures of gold, and even more important, its priceless ports on the Pacific Ocean. The sheer sweep of Sibley's proposal proved to be irresistible to Davis, who came to believe that if the campaign indeed succeeded, his new nation's highly desired recognition by the major powers in Europe would also be ensured. The only drawback to this promising scenario was the total lack of any Confederate troops who could be spared from the war's Eastern Theater. Never one to let adversity block his soaring ambition, however, newly appointed Confederate Colonel Sibley blithely assured the president that the State of Texas literally teemed with fighting men who would leap at the chance to raise the stars and bars of the Confederacy over the capital of neighboring New Mexico, and even beyond, along with the Lone Star flag of Texas, of course.

Sibley's pledge to raise his own brigade to carry out his grandiose scheme apparently proved to be the key selling point to Davis. He promptly promoted the colonel to the rank of brigadier general, wished him well on his great western adventure, and then returned to his everyday task of making his Confederacy a viable and enduring nation.

At its beginning, General Sibley's dream of a Confederate Empire in the West seemed to be coming true just as he had assured his commander-in-chief. Texas men did indeed enthusiastically rally to his cause. By the time he left San Antonio to march to New Mexico in November 1861, the general had recruited nearly four thousand men. Keen to take part in a glorious campaign to extend the Confederate cause all the way to the Pacific, and impressed with their commander's military credentials and firsthand knowledge of the land to be invaded, the men were in high spirits by the time they reached El Paso's Fort Bliss in mid-December 1861. They had trudged more than six hundred miles across desolate Texas deserts to reach their destination and to celebrate at the former federal fort located on the Rio Grande.

The Battle

Sibley's Brigade remained at Fort Bliss just long enough for the men to recover from their long march. In the process, they also managed to alienate the local population by their disorderly drunkenness and overall debauchery. To the relief of the civilians, the brigade departed El Paso in early January 1862.

The soldiers' first encounter with Union troops took place on February 17 at Fort Craig, located on the western banks of the Rio Grande some 120 miles due north of El Paso. When the Union commander of the well-fortified installation refused to order his men out of the fort to do battle, an ill and likely intoxicated Sibley chose to bypass the federal post and to continue his march north toward Albuquerque and Santa Fe. His decision to move away from Fort Craig without attempting to storm it proved costly. He was forced to discontinue his march up the verdant Rio Grande and swing far to the east and onto difficult and unforgiving terrain still known to this day as *Jornada del Muerto* (Journey of Death).

When Sibley swung his marching troops back to the Rio Grande, he encountered Union soldiers from Fort Craig who had, at last, come out to fight the invading Texans. During the ensuing Battle of Val Verde (Valverde) on February 21, 1862, neither side could claim a clear-cut victory. The cost of the conflict ran high, with Sibley's Brigade losing 36 men, and another 150 wounded. Union losses were even higher with 60 men killed in action, and 196 wounded or reported missing.

While the Union forces recovered from the brief but bloody clash, Sibley's men resumed their northward journey toward Santa Fe. Since leaving El Paso, it became apparent that Sibley's belief that the civilian population his Texans encountered along the course of their march would welcome the invaders as liberators had failed to materialize. As a result, logistics came to be the key to the success or failure of the campaign. If his troops found it possible to live off the land, Sibley could likely make it to Colorado and perhaps beyond. Failure to find adequate sustenance, though, could only foretell failure.

Somehow, the brigade's battle-weary and hungry soldiers made their way the ninety miles from Val Verde to the large town of Albuquerque, where, their commander assured them, much needed food and other essentials would be theirs for the taking. Federal troops had also moved northward and, being well aware of the logistical needs of the invaders, burned or otherwise destroyed everything of value located at Albuquerque. When the Confederates reached Santa Fe a few days later, they discovered that once again virtually everything they so badly needed had been destroyed by their enemy.

As the soldiers desperately foraged in the capital, word came that a fresh federal force of some 1300 men was en route to New Mexico from the north. That force, the 1st Colorado Volunteer Infantry commanded by Col. John P. Slough, soon encountered a small Confederate advance guard detail at Glorieta Pass, located on the Santa Fe Trail some ten miles east of the capital city. After a brief firefight, the Confederates withdrew to attain a stronger defensive position and sent for reinforcements from Santa Fe. When the fresh troops arrived on March 27, the battle was joined in deadly earnest. The rough terrain in and around the narrow canyon dictated the nature of the fighting, forcing it to take place in a series of bitter skirmishes on the steep slopes of the canyon and amid the pines and boulders that covered the mountainsides.

Col. John P. Slough, commander of the 1st Colorado Volunteer Infantry at the Battle of Glorieta Pass, became Chief Justice of New Mexico Territory after the Civil War. In December 1867, he was shot and killed in Santa Fe's La Fonda Hotel.

When the smoke of battle finally cleared in the afternoon of March 28, Confederate field commander Lt. Col. William R. Scurry believed his men had prevailed. Although the federal forces had indeed withdrawn from the field of battle, he soon learned that his initial perception of victory was sadly in error. To his dismay, the Texan commander found that a Union detail had discovered the Confederates' field supply depot and proceeded to kill all of the invaders' remount horses and pack mules, burning every one of the supply-laden wagons they found.

The battle proved to be a shallow tactical victory for the Confederates but a decisive logistical and strategic victory for the Union forces. With no supplies, no horses, little food,

The Arizona–New Mexico Campaign is more commonly known as the Sibley Campaign, named for Brig. Gen. Henry Hopkins Sibley, who led the Texas forces in an effort to secure resources and transportation routes in the West for the Confederacy. *Courtesy of Library of Congress, LC-B813-1976 A (P&P), Lot 4213.*

and precious little ammunition, Sibley's once-proud brigade had no alternative but to limp back toward Fort Bliss in defeat. Harried by Union troops all the way to El Paso, the tattered and starving Texans arrived on May 4, 1862, having experienced the loss of nearly half the original invading force. Along the way, the hapless Sibley had frequently been either too ill or reportedly too inebriated to be an effective commander. He sat out the battle at Glorieta Pass at his headquarters in Albuquerque and celebrated at great lengths upon receiving the erroneous first reports that his command had carried the day.

Sibley's soaring dreams of a Confederate Empire stretching from Richmond to San Francisco, replete with untold riches and lucrative trade routes to the Orient, had literally gone up in smoke in a narrow New Mexico canyon. Contrary to his pledge to Confederate President Davis, General Sibley had in fact managed to lose everything and gain nothing but the scorn of his own command, as well as that of many of his fellow Confederate officers.

The Texans

The Battle of Glorieta Pass, part of the larger Arizona–New Mexico Campaign, was unique among all other Civil War battles in that all participants on the Confederate side of the fray marched under the banner of the Lone Star State. To be sure, some of Sibley's Brigade hailed from other states, but for the most part the men doing the marching, enduring the privations, and in the participating in the midst of the deadly firefights were volunteers from Texas, one and all. Ineffectively commanded, poorly trained, and inadequately equipped, they suffered extraordinary losses due as much to hardships and deprivation on the march than to the bullets and artillery shells of their enemy. There can be little doubt they believed in the cause that called them to fight and die in New Mexico in the very early years of the Civil War, and their ultimate failure should not belittle their devotion to that cause.

The specific units in the New Mexico campaign were:
- Sibley's Brigade: 4th Texas Volunteer Cavalry, commanded by Col. James Reily; 5th Texas Volunteer Cavalry, commanded by Col. Tom Green; 7th Texas Volunteer

Cavalry, commanded by Col. William Steele; and Riley's Battery, commanded by Lt. John Riley.
* Baylor's Command Texas Mounted Rifles, Lt. Col. John R. Baylor; Teel's Battery, Capt. Trevanion T. Teel.

The Monument

Initially, the Texas State Historical Survey Committee (TSHSC) sought to place a state monument in the vicinity of the Glorieta Pass battlefield, but issues arising over private land ownership and differences of interpretation, eventually caused it to be relocated to Anthony, in the extreme northwest part of El Paso County, Texas, with a new focus commemorating the broader regional campaign. The dispute over the battle monument involved a wide range of characters, from politicians and Baptists to private landowners and history buffs. Central to the debate that occurred was the fact that a key physical component of the historic landscape—as it related in particular to the participation of Texas troops—was the area around Pigeon's Ranch, which in the early 1960s remained in private ownership. An alternative site seemed to be a nearby tract operated as a state monument under the auspices of the Museum of New Mexico. In April 1963, however, in a letter to TSHSC director George W. Hill, museum administrator Wayne L. Mauzy noted that because the site already had a granite marker placed by the "Daughters of the Confederacy, Texas Chapter," as well as a plaque designating the property a National Historic Landmark, "We feel that these two markers adequately commemorate the Glorieta site and that a further one might appear to be an unnecessary duplication."

At that point, the state began searching for alternative sites, and along the way, a number of key players became involved. One of the most outspoken was Gertrude Harris Cook, owner of the Glorieta Pass Studio in San Antonio, Texas. Motivated by a sense of historical accuracy, which she felt was missing from existing interpretations of the battle and the campaign, Cook became a one-person publicity campaign for the Texas monument. Her correspondence seeking support for her efforts went to such dignitaries as US Vice President Lyndon Johnson, Senator Ralph Yarborough, Senator John Tower, Representative Henry B. Gonzales, Governor John Connally, and Lieutenant Governor Preston Smith. All responded with letters of support or encouragement, but none stepped forward to resolve the situation. As a result, Cook turned her attention to the Southern Baptist Convention (SBC) encampment at Glorieta, some five miles from the battlefield, and there she found a sympathetic ear.

Cook's plan was not simple, however, and called for far more than a single monument. "So we are working to get the battlefield bought and given to the (Baptist) Assembly grounds," she wrote, "so in turn we can lease the battlefield proper as a Memorial Park, open to any state to put a monument there—in addition to a large Texas Memorial which we hope will take the form of a five pointed star—each point devoted to a hero of the battlefield; Colonel Scurry and the four who gave their lives on the field." Previously, Cook had provided additional

A mesquite tree lends little shade to the Texas monument for the Arizona–New Mexico Campaign. Located at Anthony, Texas, the monument was originally slated for the Glorieta Battlefield in New Mexico, more than three hundred miles to the north. *Courtesy of Alexander Collection.*

details of her monumental plan, noting the land she hoped the Baptists would acquire would be a place "where we can put a suitable Memorial—like at Vicksburg—and as ccstly [sic]. We have planned a structure; not like a 'front porch' as at Vicksburg, but a five pointed star with steps all around—to sit on and view the most beautiful battlfield [sic] in the world. . . ." And, being a loyal Baptist, she added a sense of urgency to her plea: "You will notice that the Methodists are building an assembly city in the Pass now. . . ."

At first, E. A. Herron, manager of the Glorieta Baptist Assembly, seemed sympathetic to a monument on the grounds, but he sought guidance from his superiors in the Sunday School Board of the SBC, acting through its Executive Council. In a split vote—there were "two members who positively opposed the idea"—the council approved the general plan for a Texas monument with three important stipulations: their members would have to approve the inscription and select the monument site, and they reserved the right to later move the monument, if they so chose, at state expense. With that understanding, James L. Sullivan of the Sunday School Board granted permission for the project to proceed. Three days later, George Hill sent an urgent telegram to Herron: "Will have to abandon plans for monument there if future contingency requiring State of Texas to pay for moving is not removed. No one including legislature can legally obligate future funds in this manner. Tomorrow is deadline. Appreciation." A note to the file dated the same day provided details of a subsequent phone call from Herron: "In re. telegram rec. this morning The Board is not willing to remove the restrictions. I'm sorry. Thank you."

With that, the planning turned to the broader story of Sibley's Campaign as it could be told along the historic route through the El Paso area. A letter went out to State Highway Engineer D. C. Greer the next day, asking for permission to place the monument at a Texas Highway Department rest area and travel information center northwest, approximately 320 miles south of Glorieta. In the letter, TSHSC president John Ben Shepperd cited a binding contractual deadline of June 25 and added, "You will recall that Sibley and Baylor's expeditions passed over the route of the highway through Anthony." On June 21, Greer formally approved the plan, authorizing his personnel to erect the monument immediately and thereby ending, at least for the twentieth century, the saga of the misplaced Glorieta monument. See the Epilogue, however, for recent developments in that regard.

Texans Remember

Three Texas counties bear names associated with the Arizona–New Mexico Campaign. Scurry County in West Texas is named for Scurry, who served with distinction in the Battle of Glorieta Pass and later died in fighting at Jenkins's Ferry, Arkansas; Tom Green County, also in West Texas, is named for Virginian Green, one of the most celebrated military men in Texas history who fought in the Texas Revolution and the Mexican War before service in the Civil War; and Val Verde County, along the Rio Grande, is named for the Battle at Val Verde in the New Mexico Territory on February 21, 1862.

Directions to Monument

North side of Texas Travel Information Center complex, 8799 S. Desert Blvd., Anthony (mile marker one exit off Interstate 10 headed east).

Suggested Readings

Alberts, Don E. *The Battle of Glorieta: Union Victory in the West.* College Station: Texas A&M University Press, 2000.

Edrington, Thomas S., and John Taylor. The *Battle of Glorieta Pass: A Gettysburg in the West, March 26–28, 1862.* Albuquerque: University of New Mexico Press, 2000.

Frazier, Donald S. *Blood and Treasure: Confederate Empire in the Southwest.* College Station: Texas A&M University Press, 1996.

Thompson, Jerry. *Civil War in the Southwest: Recollections of Sibley's Brigade.* College Station: Texas A&M University Press, 2001.

TEXAS
REMEMBERS THE VALOR AND DEVOTION OF
HER SONS WHO SERVED AT SHILOH
APRIL 6-7, 1862.

HERE THE RANGERS UPHELD THE FAME OF
THE NAME THEY BORE. THE 2ND TEXAS
FOUGHT WITH GALLANTRY AND THE 9TH
TEXAS RESPONDED TO ANY DEMAND UPON
ITS COURAGE AND ENDURANCE.

GENERAL ALBERT SIDNEY JOHNSTON OF
TEXAS GAVE HIS LIFE IN THIS BATTLE.

....

A MEMORIAL TO TEXANS
WHO SERVED IN THE CONFEDERACY

EREECTED BY THE STATE OF TEXAS 1964

Battle of Shiloh, Tennessee

Also known as Battle of Pittsburg Landing

April 6–7, 1862

The Situation

Following Maj. Gen. Ulysses S. Grant's victory at Fort Donelson, his superior officer, Maj. Gen. Henry W. Halleck, planned a Union advance down the Tennessee River. The objective of the advance was to capture the key railroad city of Corinth, Mississippi. Grant was to command the operation in the field, having barely survived efforts by Halleck to have him removed from all command responsibility. According to Grant, who became a national hero after his Donelson victory but a threatening thorn in the side of the ambitious Halleck, orders for his arrest had been issued by the army's overall commander, Gen. George B. McClellan. Only a personal intervention by US President Abraham Lincoln saved Grant's military career that now found him on the Tennessee River ready to launch a massive attack on Corinth, some 110 miles south of Fort Donelson.

Believing the Confederate forces at Corinth commanded by Gen. Albert Sidney Johnston much too firmly entrenched, Grant established his headquarters in an opulent mansion across the river from Pittsburg Landing, where his fifty thousand troops encamped, preparing for the attack on Corinth. Rather than order his sizeable army to march south immediately, Grant obeyed a direct command from General Halleck to await the arrival of thousands of reinforcements under the command of Maj. Gen. Don Carlos Buell. As Grant awaited the arrival of Buell's Army of the Ohio, General Johnston decided not to remain in the heavily fortified Corinth after all, but rather to move north to face Grant before Buell arrived. The reasons for Johnston's decision to take the initiative are not clear.

Some, including Grant himself, speculated much later that the adverse public and political opinion that had swirled around Johnston and his heretofore poor performance in the war had prompted him to move his army of forty-five thousand northward.

As Johnston moved out of Corinth, Grant continued to wait for Buell, firmly convinced the fight that was soon to come would take place at Corinth and not just across the Tennessee River from his mansion headquarters. Part of Grant's conviction in this regard perhaps stemmed from his later-expressed belief that Johnston was a vacillating and indecisive commander, not one likely to leave the relative safety of his well-defended stronghold. Grant's doubts about Johnston and his immediate plans were soon to be proved incorrect and, at least temporarily, once again damaging to his own already checkered career. Believing Pittsburg Landing, located near a rustic rural church called Shiloh, would be merely a staging point for his soon-to-be advancing army, Grant and his staff failed to implement any standard security precautions. There were no pickets posted along the two roads that led from Corinth to Grant's position, and cavalry patrols found themselves severely limited by the heavy brush that grew throughout the area.

When reports came to Grant's trusted lieutenant, Brig. Gen. William Tecumseh Sherman, that a massive force was moving toward the Union encampment, the fiery general dismissed them out of hand, failing to inform Grant of the possibility of an attack. As a result, the Union soldiers sat in camp awaiting reinforcements while Johnston, vacillating no longer, moved rapidly toward them.

The Battle

Called by some historians the first great modern battle, the horrendous clash at Shiloh was by all accounts, including Grant's, the fiercest battle fought in the Civil War's Western Theater and one with few equals in intensity in the more publicized clashes in the east. It was a battle shaped by bad weather, difficult terrain, poorly executed maneuvers by largely inexperienced combatants, and questionable generalship by both Grant and Johnston.

Maj. Gen. Lew Wallace, whose Union division took the wrong road at Shiloh and missed most of the fighting, survived both the embarrassment and the war to gain lasting fame as an author. His novel, *Ben Hur: A Tale of the Christ* is still in print.

The Union proved to be handicapped by an outmoded independent divisional command structure with its divisions led by untried generals for the most part. The Confederate force was hampered by unnecessarily delayed troop movements and, eventually, lack of adequate supplies and ammunition. At the beginning, however, the Confederates appeared likely to attain a major and much-needed victory. The Union soldiers, as well as their officers at every level, were confident that their upcoming role in the impending clash was to be strictly offensive and, as a result, were greatly surprised to find yelling rebels crashing into their campsites early on the morning of April 6.

The degree of surprise achieved by Johnston's men became a sore issue following the battle and continued to prompt heated debate for many years. Some, including Grant and Sherman, contended the Union soldiers were not taken by surprise at all, but others, namely the Northern press, saw it quite differently. A reporter for the *New York Times* claimed to be present in one camp when butternut-clad-Confederates caught their enemy completely off guard, with some soldiers casually cooking their breakfast while others still slept in their tents. As one senior Confederate general recalled after the war, he believed the Union men wore attire more fitting a bedroom than a battlefield. A British commentator on the situation called it one of the most complete surprises in the war. Another more contemporary observer made note of the fact that many Confederates, hungry from their rapid march to Shiloh, halted their advance to eat the freshly cooked breakfast dishes left behind by panic-stricken Union soldiers.

General Grant was himself eating breakfast when he heard the firing taking place across the river and quickly made his way toward the sounds of battle. To his surprise, he found his soldiers involved in a full-scale frontal attack led by General Johnston, whom he had believed to be down in Corinth safely behind his strong defensive works. Grant's army had been reduced by sickness during its encampment to the extent that Johnston now commanded a larger force. Brig. Gen. Benjamin Prentiss commanded the first Union division to fail. Inexperienced in combat, Prentiss's men broke after hours of heavy fighting and rushed back to the banks of the Tennessee, there to remain in fear or to try to swim across the river to safety on the other side. Throughout the fierce battle, thousands of other inexperienced and frightened Union soldiers fled the battle to cower at the river's edge. At one time, an estimated fifteen thousand sought relative solace at the river, unable to retreat farther. Grant soon found it necessary to establish a desertion line with a field piece placed to fire into those of his own troops who refused to rejoin the battle.

It was General Sherman's division, the least battle-tested of them all, that next caught the full fury of the Confederates. He fell back to a stronger position only to be engulfed in an intensive firefight. In time, the inexperience of the officers and the poor training of their men, combined with the brush-covered terrain, served to transform the battle from a formal, well-orchestrated and orderly clash into a series of uncoordinated bold if not foolish charges, and often deadly retreats and panicked withdrawals. The resulting casualty rate for both sides proved to be monumental and unlike anything experienced during the war to date.

Late in the afternoon of the battle's first day, a Union bullet struck General Johnston in his heel as he helped lead a less-than-enthusiastic regiment forward into battle. Not believing his wound serious enough to require medical attention, the general soon received help from his aides to dismount. In a short time, he was dead, but his death remained a guarded secret as long as possible to avoid panic among his adoring troops. Johnston was the highest-ranking officer on either side to die in battle during the entire Civil War.

Union general and division commander W. H. L. Wallace was killed shortly thereafter, and once again the tide appeared to be turning in the Confederate's favor. The surrender of General Prentiss's command of some 2,300 Union soldiers accentuated the perception of an impending Union collapse. Ironically, the logistical problems encountered in the

This elaborate monument is located near the death site of Texas commander Albert Sidney Johnston at Shiloh National Military Park, Tennessee. The loss of Johnston, considered one of the most promising military leaders on either side early in the war, proved to be a significant blow to the Confederacy. *Courtesy of Library of Congress, LC-HS503-547.*

transfer of General Prentiss and his division required several hours and virtually halted the fighting in the immediate area for about six hours. Later in the day, Confederate General P. G. T. Beauregard, who had been in command of Southern forces since the death of General Johnston, pushed his tired troops into an abortive assault against the strengthening Union positions. As night fell, and along with it torrents of rain, Beauregard rested his army.

During the night, the long awaited reinforcements commanded by General Buell arrived at the battlefield. Beauregard was apparently unaware the fresh Union troops had arrived, but following one more attempt to carry on the battle, a fierce Union counterattack wore down Confederate resolve and he ordered a retreat. Beauregard led his shattered army back down the roads to Corinth, but the expected pursuit by the victorious Union forces failed to materialize. The battle was over at last.

Repercussions about Grant's less-than-auspicious generalship prior to the battle began to surface well before the firing of the last shots. Rumors about his being drunk in his mansion were rampant, and his failure to order strong security measures combined to once again put a cloud over his career so recently revitalized by his victory at Fort Donelson. As had been the case after that successful battle, the envious General Halleck swept onto the scene and relieved Grant of command. When asked many years later about why he failed to make the obligatory report on the battle, Grant claimed Halleck refused to let him see other senior officers' reports and totally ignored him after the battle. The resilient Grant survived the public outcry about his performance, of course, as a result, once again, of the strong support of President Lincoln. The Confederacy, however, was not nearly as resilient as Grant. With its defeat at Shiloh, all possibility of regaining its lost territory in Western and Central Tennessee was forever gone.

Casualties at the Battle of Shiloh were greater than those suffered in the nation's first three wars combined.

Losses on both sides of the bloody clash were immense. Union casualties alone were reported to be more than thirteen thousand, with Confederate losses estimated to be more than ten thousand. As terrible as the losses most certainly were, Shiloh put an end to even any faint hope that the war would be a short one. As Grant saw it, the battle proved that the Union could be saved only by complete conquest of the Confederacy. It set the stage for the previously unthinkable concept of total warfare.

The Texans

Texas units at Shiloh included the following:
- 9th Texas Infantry, commanded by Col. Wright A. Stanley
- 2nd Texas Infantry, commanded by Col. John C. Moore, Lt. Col. William P. Rogers, and Maj. Hal G. Runnels
- 8th Texas Cavalry, commanded by Col. John A. Wharton

The Monument

Efforts to place monuments at key Civil War battlefields began in earnest in the early decades of the twentieth century, but some states chose not to participate at that time, often because they lacked adequate funding mechanisms or active commemorative associations. In the case of Texas, it was a matter of interpreting the state constitution, which legislators believed did not authorize state funds for monuments. So, when the Shiloh Park Commission solicited the State of Texas for a memorial on the battlefield, state officials respectfully declined. Texas was thus one of the later states to get involved in the monumentation effort. Official approval came in 1963 as part of the Civil War Centennial.

Using the standard upright tablet of Sunset Red granite used at other sites, the Texas State Historical Survey Committee approved placement along the Hamburg-Purdy Road south of the Peach Orchard and not far from the site where General Johnston died. Although within the boundaries of the national park, the monument is relatively isolated in a wooded area, which no doubt contributed to its vandalism in December 1992. Damage was limited to destruction of the bronze star that forms the centerpiece of the wreath motif near the top of the monument.

Although there were efforts to replace the star, nothing happened until 1997, soon after the Texas Historical Commission (THC) established its Military Sites Program under

The Texas monument is located along the Hamburg-Purdy Road in Shiloh National Military Park, south of the area known as the Peach Orchard. *Courtesy of Texas Historical Commission; William A. McWhorter, photographer.*

legislative mandate. On June 5 of that year, representatives of the Texas and Tennessee historical commissions gathered with National Park Service officials to witness the formal presentation of a new Lone Star for the monument. Among those making remarks at the dedication ceremony that day was Stanley O. Graves of the THC, who spoke of the long historic ties between the two states and brought the story up to date by noting his mother was a native of Tennessee and his father a son of Texas.

Texans Remember

One of the most poignant reminders of Shiloh in Texas is the recumbent marble effigy of Johnston, carved by the noted sculptor, Elisabet Ney, in the State Cemetery in Austin. Enclosed by a metal and glass grave house that features ornate Victorian detailing, it is a focal point of the historic burial ground.

Although several Official Texas Historical Markers mention Johnston, two are of particular interest:

- Southwest of Edna (Jackson County) via state and local roads is a monument from 1936 that marks the site of a duel between Johnston and Gen. Felix Huston on February 5, 1837, in which Johnston was severely wounded.
- On FM 1521 in the Brazoria County community of Bonney is a marker commemorating the site of Johnston's plantation, China Grove.

Directions to Monument

Hamburg-Purdy Road, Shiloh National Military Park. Ask at the visitor center for specific directions within the park.

Suggested Readings

Cunningham, O. Edward, Gary Joiner, and Timothy B. Smith, eds. *Shiloh and the Western Campaign of 1862*. New York: Savas Beatie, 2007.

Groom, Winston. *Shiloh, 1862*. Washington, DC: National Geographic Society, 2012.

Smith, Timothy B. *The Untold Story of Shiloh: The Battle and the Battlefield*. Knoxville: University of Tennessee Press, 2008.

————. *This Great Battlefield of Shiloh: History, Memory, and the Establishment of a Civil War National Military Park*. Knoxville: University of Tennessee Press, 2006.

Woodworth, Steven E., ed. *The Shiloh Campaign*. Carbondale: Southern Illinois University Press, 2009.

TEXAS

REMEMBERS THE VALOR AND DEVOTION OF
ITS SOLDIERS WHO PARTICIPATED IN THE BATTLE
OF GAINES' MILL, VIRGINIA – JUNE 27, 1862.

HERE, CONFEDERATE GEN. ROBERT E. LEE
CONTINUED HIS ATTACKS AGAINST UNION MAJ.
GEN. GEORGE B. McCLELLAN'S ARMY OF THE
POTOMAC WHICH WAS ATTEMPTING TO CAPTURE
RICHMOND. FROM JUNE 25-JULY 1, LEE AND
McCLELLAN FOUGHT A SERIES OF ENGAGEMENTS
KNOWN AS THE SEVEN DAYS BATTLES, THIS BEING
THE 3RD IN THAT SERIES. ON JUNE 27,
McCLELLAN'S V CORPS UNDER BRIG. GEN. FITZ
JOHN PORTER HELD A STRONG DEFENSIVE
POSITION BEHIND BOATSWAIN'S CREEK ON
TURKEY HILL. LEE ORDERED AN ALL-OUT
ASSAULT, PERHAPS THE LARGEST HE EVER
ACHIEVED, HOPING TO SEND NEARLY 60,000
MEN ACROSS A TWO-MILE FRONT. FOR OVER FIVE
HOURS, PORTER'S MEN REPULSED LEE'S
ATTACKS. NEAR SUNDOWN, LEE SENT FORWARD
BRIG. GEN. W.H.C. WHITING'S DIVISION,
COMPOSED OF BRIG. GEN. JOHN BELL HOOD'S
TEXAS BRIGADE AND COL. EVANDER LAW'S
BRIGADE. ON THIS GROUND, HOOD PERSONALLY
LED THE 4TH TEXAS AND SPEARHEADED THE
ATTACK. THEY WERE CLOSELY SUPPORTED BY
THE 18TH GEORGIA. HOOD'S BAYONET ASSAULT
BROKE THE UNION LINE DRIVING PORTER'S
MEN FROM THEIR BREASTWORKS ON THE HIGH
GROUND. THE OTHER REGIMENTS OF HOOD'S
BRIGADE EMERGED FROM THE WOODS, AND UNION
RESISTANCE COLLAPSED. PORTER'S CORPS
RETREATED ACROSS THE CHICKAHOMINY RIVER,
GIVING LEE THE FIRST VICTORY OF HIS CAREER AS
A GENERAL. UNNERVED BY THE DEFEAT,
McCLELLAN NOW FOCUSED ON SAVING HIS ARMY
AS LEE CONTINUED HIS ATTACKS THROUGH JULY 1.
THE TEXAS UNITS, TOGETHER WITH THE
GEORGIANS AND SOUTH CAROLINIANS IN THE
BRIGADE, AND PLAYED DECISIVE ROLES IN
ACHIEVING McCLELLAN'S DEFEAT AND SAVING
THE CONFEDERATE CAPITAL FROM CAPTURE.

ERECTED BY THE STATE OF TEXAS 2012

Battle of Gaines' Mill, Virginia

Also known as First Battle of Cold Harbor or Battle of the Chickahominy River

April 6–7, 1862

The Situation

Nearly three months after Maj. Gen. Ulysses S. Grant's combined fights with the Confederates at Shiloh, as well as with his commanding officer, Maj. Gen. Henry W. Halleck, a new military leader rose to the top in the Confederate Army. His name was Gen. Robert E. Lee, a onetime colonel in the US Army who resigned that commission to devote himself to serving first his native Virginia and then the Confederate States of America. Lee served his new nation in various positions with lesser responsibility before being chosen to assume command of the Army of Northern Virginia by President Jefferson Davis on June 1, 1862. He succeeded Gen. Joseph E. Johnston, who had been seriously wounded by shrapnel the day before during the Battle of Seven Pines.

When Lee took command, his army, and indeed the entire Confederate cause, was in imminent peril. The Union Army, commanded by Gen. George B. McClellan had come to within ten miles of the Confederate capital city of Richmond, Virginia, and close enough to hear the city's church bells. The Union commander had been US President Abraham Lincoln's choice to succeed the aging Winfield Scott, hero of the Mexican War, as general-in-chief of the entire federal army. Once in top command, McClellan quickly proved to be a problem to the beleaguered president. Excessively vain and enormously self-centered, the new general-in-chief was soon publicly disdainful of Lincoln's entire war organization in Washington, DC, and particularly openly contemptuous of the president himself.

Even as a large Confederate force continued to occupy the region around the scene of its victory at the First Battle of Manassas, a short distance from Washington, McClellan spent his time parading his soldiers in glorious reviews and then galloping past his cheering and adoring troops with hat raised in a dramatic gesture of salute. In addition to his talent for showmanship, McClellan, frequently called "The Young Napoleon" with good reason, was also an excellent organizer, a thorough trainer, and capable of designing great strategic military plans that he conceived to bring the Civil War to a quick and victorious conclusion. As he saw it, he alone had what it would take to achieve such a magnificent goal. The problem lurking within all of McClellan's plans was that they were not based on strategic reality. This fault, coupled with his chronic inability to get his army into motion to at least attempt to consummate his plans, made his claim of being a military genius suspect in short order.

Referring to his battle wound that led to the appointment of Robert E. Lee as his successor, Gen. Joseph E. Johnston remarked, "The shot that struck me down is the very best that has been fired for the Southern cause yet."

Once in the field, McClellan also possessed an uncanny ability to grossly overestimate the size of the enemy force that his own plans had called for him to face. Rather than push his idolizing troops into battle with this imagined horde, he chose to delay and dither, all the while loudly blaming President Lincoln and War Secretary Edwin Stanton of deliberately withholding the tens of thousands of soldiers he believed he needed to even begin to match the enemy's numbers. On one occasion, highly agitated, he accused his civilian superiors in Washington of treason. Remarkably, President Lincoln, hard pressed to find the general the nation so sorely needed, let the accusation pass with neither comment nor disciplinary action. Until he found the right general, McClellan would have to do.

Displaying immense forbearance and patience, Lincoln pushed and prodded the young general to hasten his training regimen, ensure the safety of the nation's capital from incursions by the Southern force encamped at Manassas less than thirty miles from it, and to devise a realistic plan to move aggressively against the rebels to sweep away all opposition by conquering the Confederate capital at Richmond, located just one hundred miles south of Washington. An imaginative planner and anything but an aggressive doer, McClellan soon presented Lincoln with a bold move that would take the Confederates by complete surprise to conquer Richmond and thus quickly end the war. Further, he would accomplish all of this but also spare his by now huge army the travails of a long march through Virginia. He would, he explained to a dubious Lincoln in February 1862, move his army southward by sea.

In what came to be known as the Peninsular Campaign, McClellan envisioned moving his entire 150,000-man army down the Potomac River, out into Chesapeake Bay, and then landing in eastern Virginia and marching westward to take Richmond. In the process he would flank the 35,000-man Confederate force still at Manassas, divide the enemy's armies, easily win the war, and become the national hero he had long believed he was predestined to become.

Following a successful boat journey to Virginia's coast, McClellan encountered a far stronger resistance east of Richmond than he had anticipated, mainly as a result of General Johnston's hasty march away from Manassas to confront the Union Army as it moved up the Yorktown Peninsula upon disembarking from the troop ships. The first significant clash during McClellan's optimistic march toward Richmond took place on May 31, 1862, at Seven Pines. It was during this fierce fight that left General Johnston severely wounded. It was also where McClellan's plan began to fall victim to the realization that there were far more Confederate soldiers in front of him than he could possibly defeat.

Despite his growing fear of becoming insurmountably outnumbered, McClellan kept moving, albeit cautiously, toward Richmond. On June 26, in the second day of what came to be called the Seven Days Battles, General Lee launched his newly named Army of Northern Virginia in a furious attack against McClellan's far larger force. Greatly aided by intelligence gained during J. E. B. Stuart's audacious cavalry maneuver that completely encircled McClellan's army, Lee determined the key weaknesses in his enemy's position that would enable the Confederates to protect their capital from siege and likely capitulation. In what his biographer termed the general's first major Civil War victory, the Battle of Gaines' Mill was then set to commence.

The Battle

The Union's opening position at Gaines' Mill on June 27 seemed to be strong. The site's principal natural feature was a plateau averaging between eighty and ninety feet in height. At its base was a wide steam that ran about six feet deep with three lines of breastworks at the base of the plateau. On its summit was what one observer termed a bristling crown of artillery. A total Union effective force of forty thousand men was at or near the site, all under the command of Brig. Gen. Fitz John Porter.

Brig. Gen. D. H. Hill and Maj. Gen. James Longstreet initially led the Confederate assault on the formidable natural fortress. Although late to the battle, Maj. Gen. Thomas J. (Stonewall) Jackson arrived with an army fatigued by a forced march from a successful campaign in the Shenandoah Valley that had greatly reduced the Union pressure on Richmond. Jackson's delayed arrival held up Lee's full-scale attack until late afternoon, although a previous brief assault had set the battle in motion. After two hours of exchanges of artillery fire and infantry feints, little had been accomplished by either side.

According to historian Douglas Southall Freeman, the soldiers of Hood's Texas Brigade were "Man for man, perhaps the best combat troops in the Army [of Northern Virginia]."

As the day drew to a close, the always-aggressive Lee ordered a full charge up the plateau with Longstreet and Hill pushing against the flanks of the breastworks, and the commands of generals John Bell Hood and Evander Law hurling their way upward to attack the Union center. Although most sources credit Hood's Texas

Brigade as being the first to breach the Union lines, a few historians claim the Union center was pierced in force by the combined effort of several units. The Union position gave way as its defenders fled from the breastworks and batteries in what soon became a rout. The repulse of a final and foolishly suicidal US cavalry charge brought the battle to its close. Lee had won what would be his first fight of the war, which would continue for nearly three more years. McClellan had, as usual, acted defensively and attempted nothing that might have altered the battle. As a result of his defeat, he began an embarrassing retreat from what he had hoped would be his crowning glory. He would face Lee again, but this first encounter must surely have added fuel to his growing fear of defeat.

The cost of Lee's victory was dear. His Army of Northern Virginia suffered 8,750 casualties, whereas McClellan recorded losses of just fewer than 7,000. At the battle's end, Lee wired Confederate President Davis the good news of victory. After five hours of severe fighting, Richmond was, for the time being at least, safe from Union occupation.

The Texans

The Texas troops directly involved in the Battle of Gaines' Mill were all part of General Hood's Texas Brigade. Specific units were:
- 1st Texas Volunteer Regiment
- 4th Texas Volunteer Infantry Regiment
- 5th Texas Volunteer Infantry Regiment

The Monument

Dedicated in May 2012, the monument at Gaines' Mill is the newest in the Texas Historical Commission's (THC) Civil War series. Although many individuals and organizations contributed to the cost of the monument, it was the leadership of the Hood's Texas Brigade Association, Re-activated, that made the project possible. Surviving members of Hood's Texas Brigade formed the original association in 1872, and the veterans continued to meet on a regular basis until 1933, when only two attended the meeting. The association thus deactivated, but in 1966 it began again, this time as an organization of veterans' descendants.

Working in partnership to interpret within a complex and dispersed battlefield landscape the key role Texas forces played in the conflict at Gaines' Mill, representatives of Hood's Texas Brigade Association, Re-activated, the THC, and the Richmond Battlefields Association (RBA) considered several locations, all within close proximity to each other. In the end, though, the decision was to tell the Texas story at a site along Boatswain's Creek on private land owned by the RBA. It was there the Texans under Hood spearheaded the Confederate advance on the day of battle, crossing the stream and rushing up Turkey Hill to bust the Union line, thereby setting in motion the collapse of the federal position on the hill. Those who worked to determine the right location for the Texas monument believe its presence will help open new areas of the battlefield for interpretation, while also providing heritage tourists with a renewed appreciation for one of the most celebrated fighting units of the Lone Star State.

William A. McWhorter, military sites program coordinator with the Texas Historical Commission, speaks at the dedication of the Gaines' Mill monument in 2012. *Courtesy of Texas Historical Commission; Lisa Avra, photographer.*

A crowd gathered at the site on May 19, 2012, to dedicate the monument. Present were dignitaries from Virginia and Texas, as well as representatives of both the THC and the RBA. As the ceremony got underway, a small plane flew overhead trailing a replica of the Beauregard Confederate battle flag followed by a banner that read, "I SALUTE THE CONFEDERATE FLAG." The flyover, evidently targeting what the protesters believed to be a lack of adequate Civil War commemoration efforts by the State of Virginia during the sesquicentennial of the conflict, served also as a reminder that debate over the war and its interpretation continues.

Texans Remember

Various historical markers in Texas reference individuals who participated in the fighting at Gaines' Mill and returned to the state to become productive citizens. There are markers, too, that mention either Hood or his noted Texas Brigade. One such marker in Granbury, as one might expect, tells the story of Hood as the namesake of Hood County in North Central Texas (courthouse square). There are also a number of markers commemorating early annual gatherings of brigade veterans such as the 1906 reunion at Somerville, Burleson County (SH 6, N side of town); the 1912 event, held in the Calvert Baptist Church,

As the dedication ceremony for the Gaines' Mill monument got underway, a small plane flew overhead trailing a banner in support of the Confederacy, a clear indication of the strong emotions that still surround efforts to interpret the Civil War. *Courtesy of Texas Historical Commission; Lisa Avra, photographer.*

Calvert, Robertson County (Elm and Burnett); and the 1914 event at Temple, Bell County (111 N. Main), a town not in existence until years after the Civil War. There are also a number of markers that speak to the recruitment of men for the brigade, such as the one in Independence, Washington County, for formation of Company I of the 5th Texas Infantry, the Texas Aides (FM 390).

Although such markers are understandable, given the veneration of Hood's Texas Brigade through the years, there are other markers that present a slight twist on the usual story. The one for Capt. Isaac Newton Moreland Turner (b. 1839), buried in the Turner Cemetery about twenty miles east of Livingston, in Polk County, tells of a Georgia native who moved to East Texas before the war and became a successful planter. Enlisting local men for the Confederacy in 1861, he became the youngest company commander in Hood's brigade. Killed in fighting near Suffolk, Virginia, in 1863, he was buried on his ancestral land in Georgia. However, because it was always his wish to be buried in his adopted home state, his remains were finally reinterred in Polk County in 1994, more than 130 years after his death.

Another Hood-related marker with a strange twist is that of Alabama-born Mollie A. Bailey, a traveling entertainer with her husband, Gus, before the war. When he and his brother joined Hood's Texas Brigade, Mollie went along as a nurse and, as the historical marker at her grave in Houston's Hollywood Cemetery notes, a "member of Hood's minstrels, entertaining the troops." A marker for Gus in the small Hill County town of Blum, provides another glimpse of Mollie's wartime exploits with the intriguing line that she "smuggled notes and quinine past enemy in her hair." In the years following the war, the couple became successful circus owners, with Mollie in later years recognized as the "Circus Queen of the Southwest." She died in Houston in 1918.

Directions to Monument

Marker is accessible via the 6300 block of Watt House Road (Virginia 718), 0.4 miles south of Cold Harbor Road, Mechanicsville.

Suggested Readings

Burton, Brian K. *Extraordinary Circumstances: The Seven Days Battles*. Bloomington: Indiana University Press, 2010.

Gallagher, Gary W. *The Richmond Campaign of the Peninsula and the Seven Days*. Chapel Hill: University of North Carolina Press, 2008.

Sprull, Matt, III, and Matt Sprull, IV. *Echoes of Thunder: A Guide to the Seven Days Battles*. Knoxville: University of Tennessee Press, 2006.

TEXAS

REMEMBERS THE VALOR AND DEVOTION OF HER
SOLDIERS WHO PARTICIPATED IN THE BATTLE OF
SECOND MANASSAS, VIRGINIA—AUGUST 28-30, 1862.

ON THIS FIELD, CONFEDERATE GEN. ROBERT E. LEE'S
ARMY OF NORTHERN VIRGINIA WON THE DECISIVE
BATTLE OF THE NORTHERN VIRGINIA CAMPAIGN
AGAINST UNION MAJ. GEN. JOHN POPE'S ARMY OF
VIRGINIA. ARRIVING ON THE SECOND DAY, AUGUST
29TH, CONFEDERATE MAJ. GEN. JAMES LONGSTREET'S
WING TOOK POSITION OPPOSITE POPE'S LEFT FLANK.
LATE THAT AFTERNOON BRIG. GEN. JOHN BELL
HOOD'S TEXAS BRIGADE SAW ITS FIRST COMBAT OF
THE ENGAGEMENT, ADVANCING INTO THE UNION
LINE. AT GROVETON, THEIR POSITION UNTENABLE,
THE BRIGADE WITHDREW THE FOLLOWING MORNING.
MISINTERPRETING CONFEDERATE MANEUVERS AS A
RETREAT, GEN. POPE ORDERED ANOTHER ATTACK ON
GEN. STONEWALL JACKSON'S POSITION ON AUGUST 30TH.
WITH THE HELP OF GEN. LONGSTREET'S ARTILLERY, THE
UNION ATTACK WAS REPULSED. GEN. LONGSTREET'S FIVE
DIVISIONS THEN COUNTERATTACKED IN ONE OF THE
LARGEST, SIMULTANEOUS MASS ASSAULTS OF THE
WAR. HOOD'S TEXAS BRIGADE LED THE ADVANCE
WITH THE ENTIRE WING PIVOTING ON THE BRIGADE.
IN THE ENSUING COMBAT HOOD'S TEXAS BRIGADE
OVERWHELMED THE 5TH AND 10TH NEW YORK ZOUAVES
AT GROVETON AND DROVE OFF A BRIGADE OF
PENNSYLVANIA RESERVES. THEIR EFFORTS CLIMAXED
WITH THE CAPTURE OF KERN'S PENNSYLVANIA
BATTERY. ALTHOUGH THE TERRAIN AND STUBBORN
UNION RESISTANCE ON CHINN RIDGE ULTIMATELY
BROKE THE TACTICAL INTEGRITY OF THE UNIT,
THE TEXAS BRIGADE CONTRIBUTED SIGNIFICANTLY
TO THE COLLAPSE OF THE UNION LEFT FLANK WHICH
FORCED POPE'S RETREAT THAT NIGHT AND OPENED
THE WAY FOR LEE'S INVASION OF MARYLAND.

ERECTED BY THE STATE OF TEXAS 2012

Battle of Second Manassas, Virginia

Also known as Second Battle of Bull Run

August 28–30, 1862

The Situation

By late summer 1862, the leadership of the fledgling Confederate nation could allow itself a mighty sigh of relief. The Union's controversial Gen. George B. McClellan, whose forces had come to within close-hailing distance of the Confederacy's capital city of Richmond, Virginia, had been relieved of command by US President Abraham Lincoln. His army had been ordered away from the gates of the city with instructions to fall back to Washington. McClellan, a master military strategist and motivator but wholly inept at making his army move forward, had fallen victim to his personal demons of excessive cautiousness, indecisiveness, and timidity. More important, however, he had also been embarrassingly outsmarted and dramatically outgeneraled by the South's newly appointed Eastern Theater commander, Gen. Robert E. Lee. A little more than a year previous, Lee had declined an offer to take command of all Union forces. Instead, he had resigned his commission as a colonel in the US Army to cast his lot with the army of his beloved Commonwealth of Virginia then, by extension, soon after with the Confederate States of America.

When Joseph E. Johnston, the South's commanding general in the East, fell wounded at Seven Pines in May 1862, Lee became his successor. The shot that felled Johnston was, in his own estimation, the best shot fired on behalf of the Confederacy during the entire Civil

War. When Lee proceeded to win six of his first seven battles, Johnston's assertion proved to be valid. The Confederacy had clearly found the general who would sustain it on many fields of battle for the next three tumultuous years.

The Union, on the other hand, was as yet unable to find anyone to match Lee's brilliance. Although vastly superior to its enemy in both manpower and matériel, the North seemed curiously incapable of finding a general who could capitalize on his country's bountiful assets and put them to good use against the foe. Lincoln, arguably the most engaged commander-in-chief to occupy the White House for the next eighty years, possessed an innate grasp of the nation's strategic overview but finding the right general to implement his vision proved elusive. Finally losing patience with the always-dithering McClellan as the general tiptoed toward Richmond, Lincoln turned next to Maj. Gen. John Pope, a bombastic and boastful officer who had shown at least some degree of aggressiveness in various battles in the Western Theater. Pope had served with distinction in the Mexican War and later been an engineering officer on the wild prairies of Texas, where he left his name on such-now disappeared sites as Pope's Wells and Pope's Camp.

Upon coming east to assume command of the now leaderless and frazzled Union forces in Virginia, General Pope managed to alienate the affections of the men he soon had to command, as well as those of the senior officers over whom he had been promoted despite their superiority in date of rank. In his post-bellum report on the situation, Pope made much of his reluctance to accept the senior command position, claiming that he repeatedly begged both President Lincoln and General-in-Chief Henry W. Halleck to allow him to stay out west. The recorded reaction of many of those officers he superseded, however, indicates that Pope actually more than relished his unusual ascendancy to the topmost command position in the war's most critical crucible.

Somewhere along the way, the boastful Pope had also earned the disfavor of General Lee, the man he was soon to face in a highly significant battle. Even though the usually even-tempered and highly self-controlled Southern general seldom spoke ill of any man, be he friend or foe, Lee described Pope as being a "miscreant," clearly welcoming an opportunity to match wits with him on the battlefield.

That opportunity came soon after Pope took command of the restructured and newly named Army of Virginia. Lincoln charged Pope's army to defend the federal capital at Washington at all costs while at the same time bringing the North's superiority in manpower to bear on General Lee before he could do any further damage to the Union cause. To aid Pope in his daunting, but well-defined, mission, Lincoln appointed generals Irvin McDowell and Fitz John Porter. The former was the ill-fated officer who had been embarrassed and thoroughly trounced just a year previously at what would later be known as the First Battle of Manassas. The latter, General Porter, had only recently been outmaneuvered by General Lee at the Battle of Gaines' Mill.

Likely assuming that his enemy would continue to cling to its previously announced strategy of maintaining only a defensive posture in the war and seemingly content to merely keep Union forces out of its heartland, Pope vigorously set out to test that strategy by moving aggressively southward. His intention was to capture the key capital city of Richmond, the prize so recently denied General McClellan. That McClellan had so gloriously failed to accomplish this goal only served to greatly motivate Pope who disliked "Little Mac" every bit as much as the recently deposed McClellan despised him. With President Lincoln's ever-present fears for the safety of the nation's capital somewhat allayed by the leaving behind of a large defensive contingent, Pope set out to conquer Richmond, defeat Lee, bring the Civil War to a swift and satisfactory conclusion, and further humiliate McClellan—but not necessarily in that order. What Pope did not know, at least not yet, was that General Lee was no ordinary commander. Having not the slightest inclination to stand fast in defense of Richmond, the audacious Lee sought rather to carry the war directly toward those who would dare lay waste to Virginia's precious soil and destroy the Confederacy in the process.

> When he was with the US Army Topographical Engineers in 1855, working to select a railroad route across West Texas, Capt. John Pope established a water drilling camp in present Loving County—one of the first drilling operations in the region. Much of the small outpost was later inundated by the waters of Red Bluff Reservoir.

To put his newly conceived but untested offensive strategy in motion, Lee needed three supporting elements to be in place. First, he required a secure base from which to operate. To ensure this, he created a formidable series of elaborate entrenchments to protect Richmond. Next, he needed a quick infusion of manpower, and this he obtained by recalling Maj. Gen. Thomas J. (Stonewall) Jackson from his successful diversionary campaign in the Shenandoah Valley. Finally, Lee had to know exactly where General Pope and his incoming reinforcements were at all times and how many men made up the Union force. Once again, he turned to the colorful Maj. Gen. J. E. B. Stuart and his fast-riding cavalry to provide him with the vital intelligence he required.

With General Jackson moving rapidly south from the valley and with Maj. Gen. James Longstreet's five divisions nearly ready to move forward against Pope's advancing force, Lee needed only to learn from Stuart the position and progress of Pope's army. With that key information in hand, General Lee prepared to spring the tactical trap that would in time be known as the Second Battle of Manassas.

The Battle

Unconventional perhaps even to a fault, Lee, now in full command of the Army of Northern Virginia, defied all standard military doctrines by dividing his forces as he moved against Pope rather than concentrating his manpower for maximum effectiveness. He sent orders to Jackson, en route from the north, to circle behind the main body of Pope's army. He then directed Longstreet to move his divisions on a northerly course to confront Pope directly. Longstreet complied with Lee's orders with what had become his customary deliberation, while Jackson's so-called foot cavalry moved rapidly southward toward Pope's rear.

On August 25, after a series of skirmishes along their route of march, Jackson's men arrived at the rear of Pope's army having trudged more than fifty miles in less than thirty-six hours. Much to the delight of the weary troops, they easily captured the burgeoning Union supply depot and railroad junction point at Manassas Junction, some twenty miles south of Washington. This occupation not only cut Pope's main logistical supply rail line but also provided Jackson's hungry marchers with copious quantities of long-denied delicacies such as pickled oysters, Havana cigars, and when the dour and abstemious Jackson was not looking, seemingly limitless barrels of rum and wine. After eating and drinking all they could hold and packing away that which could not be immediately consumed, the men torched whatever remained.

General Pope, understandably outraged upon hearing of this violation of his supposedly well-guarded key supply depot, turned his full attention to the capture of the culprit responsible for it, the already-legendary Stonewall Jackson. In keeping with his own ground rule to always mystify the enemy, however, the elusive Jackson had simply disappeared from the view of Pope's scouts but was reportedly somewhere near the site of the lamentable Union defeat at the First Battle of Manassas in 1861. When Pope eventually found Jackson's men awaiting him hidden in an abandoned railroad cut, the fierce battle began. As the fight raged on, Pope, who had been waging a disorganized and sporadic sort of firefight, suddenly came to realize that his army was in a precarious position. Blindly intent on destroying the mythic Jackson, Pope ignored his own scouts' repeated warnings that Longstreet's huge force would soon be arriving on the battle scene, thus effectively entrapping the bulk of Pope's army between the fiercely fighting men of Jackson's command and the fresh multitude being led by Longstreet, with Lee riding with him.

Lee, possessed of an almost uncanny ability to divine what his foes were likely to do in almost every situation, correctly anticipated Pope's overeagerness to defeat Jackson and his resulting blindness to the changing scene on the field brought about by Longstreet's arrival. Pope continued to fight on gamely, but with nearly disastrous results. At one point, he launched a major frontal attack against what he had somehow imagined to be a retreating Jackson. When it developed that the Confederate commander was actually merely repositioning some elements of his command for a flanking maneuver rather than retreating, the carnage inflicted on Pope's attackers proved to be severe. The imagined retreat, however, served to convince Pope that the Confederates were actually withdrawing from the field. This conviction prompted him to send a message to Washington proclaiming victory in the battle. A heavy barrage from Longstreet's massed artillery quickly disabused Pope of any thoughts of victory, and on August 30 it was the Union Army that withdrew, its defeated generals once again slinking back into Washington to face a disturbed and disappointed President Lincoln.

It had been a short-but-vicious three-day fight. Once again, Brig. Gen. John Bell Hood's Texas Brigade had been in the thick of it. The key collapse of the Union left flank at Chinn Ridge, brought about by Hood, was a major factor in Pope's retreat at the end of the battle. One Texan, a veteran of the fight, later recalled seeing a great number of brightly uniformed bodies of fallen New York Zouaves strewn across a field when the shooting stopped. Their red and blue uniforms, he wrote, reminded him of Texas wildflowers blooming in the springtime.

There were many other bodies to be found on the battlefield. Of the sixty thousand men Pope led to Manassas, sixteen thousand had fallen. Of Lee's combined fifty thousand-man force, roughly nine thousand became casualties. In total, the casualty rate at Second Manassas was five times greater than that of the first battle at the same site in 1861.

When the smoke of battle cleared, Pope was defeated but still convinced of his ability to lead men in combat. In his colorful and understandably totally self-serving postwar account of the fight, he argued that many others should be blamed for the defeat. In some ways he was correct. Rancor among the generals prohibited any significant transfer of troops that might have changed the course of battle, but it is more than likely that Pope's poor generalship was the single most significant cause of the Union defeat.

Pope did find reason to initiate court-martial proceedings against General Porter, who had failed to obey an order to hurl his men into a direct head-on confrontation with Longstreet's clearly superior legions. Found guilty, Porter was exonerated sixteen years later by a board that rendered the opinion that by ignoring Pope's foolish order, Porter had saved hundreds of lives.

Regardless of how General Pope perceived his performance at Second Manassas, it is clear he earned the enmity of President Lincoln and the federal war department. Soon after the fight, he was relieved of command and sent back to the west he so greatly admired, but not as a combat general. Instead, his superiors dispatched him to the relative wilds of Minnesota, there to serve, with some distinction, in the ongoing efforts to pacify the warlike Sioux. Pope remained in the army even after the Sioux proved on the Little Bighorn in Montana that they were far from being pacified. In 1883, he received promotion to major general in the regular army, his epic failure at Second Manassas apparently forgiven if not forgotten.

Pope's most haunting memory of that battle was likely not his exile to Minnesota but the news of his replacement in Virginia after Second Manassas. As Pope rode in disgrace into Washington, a diminutive figure rode out to rally the shattered Army of Virginia. A mighty roar arose from the suddenly reinvigorated Union ranks. Little Mac was back in command.

Meanwhile, the victorious Lee took stock of the Confederate situation after the battle. Promptly, and with the initially somewhat reluctant concurrence of President Jefferson Davis, Lee came to the conclusion that the moment had come for his Army of Northern Virginia to immediately and aggressively abandon the previous defensive strategy and instead carry the war away from the torn battlefields of Virginia and onto the enemy's turf. Emboldened by his recent victory, he would now cross the Potomac, avoid the strongly defended citadel that Washington had become, and invade the land of the enemy to do battle as soon as possible.

Perhaps the most fitting tribute to the significant Battle of Second Manassas came from the pen of the general who lost the encounter. Long after the war ended, Pope wrote, with more than a glimmer of admiration, that by moving away from his defensive lines at the Confederate capital city, Lee had actually chosen between the danger of losing Richmond and the chance of capturing Washington. The fact that within two months after taking command, Lee had pushed the opposing federal army from its position less than twenty miles in front of Richmond to a new position slightly more than twenty miles below Washington makes it clear that Lee, the bold gambler, had made the right decision.

Outside the boundaries of Manassas National Battlefield Park in a densely wooded area on private land inaccessible to the public is a stone monument believed to mark the battlefield death site and possible burial site of young Timothy Lincoln Dunklin (b. 1841), who served with Company E of the 4th Texas Infantry from Waco.

The Texans

General Hood's Brigade consisted mainly of Texas units during the Battle of Second Manassas. The specific units making up the brigade were:

- 1st Texas Volunteer Infantry Regiment
- 4th Texas Volunteer Infantry Regiment
- 5th Texas Volunteer Infantry Regiment

The Monument

Texas Historical Commission (THC) and National Park Service (NPS) representatives helped dedicate the new monument in 2012 on land outside the national battlefield near Chinn Ridge. The THC and the Civil War Trust worked in partnership to secure the site and preserve it for future interpretive efforts, including future donation to the NPS. Such private–public partnerships often result in additions to the nation's battlefield stock where other funds are not readily available. Because the Civil War Trust has battlefield preservation as its central goal, it is fitting that they have played such an integral role in helping interpret the story of the Texans who served at Second Manassas.

Texans Remember

Jackson County in the lush Texas coastal plains is named for President Andrew Jackson, but a county four hundred miles to the northwest in rugged West Texas is named for General Stonewall Jackson. Stonewall County, with Aspermont as its seat of government, honors the military leadership of the general under whom many Texas forces fought during the Second Battle of Manassas. The small Gillespie County town of Stonewall, near which Lyndon B. Johnson grew up, is also named for the general.

The man who gave Jackson his famous sobriquet during the fighting at First Manassas and who was later mortally wounded in that battle was Brig. Gen. Barnard Elliott Bee, Jr., the namesake of Bee County and its county seat, Beeville, also in the coastal plains. Out west on the state's high plains is the county of Upton, named for two brothers who

The slab of Texas Sunset Red granite that became the Second Manassas monument undergoes preparation work at Stasswender Memorials in Austin, Texas, 2012. *Courtesy of Texas Historical Commission; Jim Stasswender, photographer.*

were Confederate colonels in service from their adopted state of Texas: William F. Upton, who fought at Galveston, and John Cunningham Upton, killed in the fighting at Second Manassas.

Directions to Monument

Near Chinn Ridge Loop off Sudley Road, south of the Lee Highway (US 29), Manassas. Inquire at the Henry Hill Visitor Center, Manassas Battlefield National Park, 6511 Sudley Road, for specific directions.

Suggested Readings

Hennessey, John. *Return to Bull Run: The Campaign and Battle of Second Manassas.* New York: Simon and Schuster, 1993.

Patchan, Scott C., and John Hennessey. *Second Manassas: Longstreet's Attack and the Struggle for Chinn Ridge.* Washington, DC: Potomac Books, 2011.

TEXAS

REMEMBERS THE VALOR AND DEVOTION OF
ITS SOLDIERS WHO PARTICIPATED IN THE BATTLE
OF RICHMOND, KENTUCY—AUGUST 29 & 30, 1862.

HERE, CONFEDERATE MAJ. GEN. EDMUND KIRBY
SMITH LED HIS NEWLY ORGANIZED CONFEDERATE
ARMY OF KENTUCKY IN AN EFFORT TO FORCE THE
UNION ARMY OUT OF THE REGION AND
THEREBY OPEN AN AVENUE TO THE NORTH. AS THE
BATTLE BECAME MORE INVOLVED, A CONCENTRATED
ASSAULT BY COL. THOMAS McCRAY'S BRIGADE—PART
OF BRIG. GEN. THOMAS CHURCHILL'S DIVISION AND
MADE UP PRIMARILY OF TEXAS DISMOUNTED
CAVALRY REGIMENTS—STRUCK THE VULNERABLE
RIGHT FLANK OF FEDERAL BRIG. GEN. MAHLON D.
MANSON'S LINE OF BATTLE. THIS ATTACK FROM
A HIDDEN RAVINE, NOW KNOWN AS CHURCHILL'S
DRAW, FORCED THE ENTIRE FEDERAL LINE TO
COLLAPSE AND A CONFUSED FEDERAL RETREAT
NORTHWARD ENSUED. THIS ACTION WAS JUST THE
BEGINNING OF A SERIES OF CONSECUTIVE
VICTORIES FOR CONFEDERATE FORCES THAT DAY.
THESE TEXAS DISMOUNTED CAVALRY REGIMENTS
AND DOUGLAS'S 1ST TEXAS ARTILLERY PLAYED
PIVOTAL ROLES IN VICIOUS FIGHTING AT
DUNCANNON ROAD AND IN THE RICHMOND
CEMETERY LATER IN THE DAY. THESE ENGAGE-
MENTS PRODUCED ONE OF THE CONFEDERACY'S
MOST RESOUNDING VICTORIES, AND THESE TEXAS
UNITS PLAYED DECISIVE ROLES IN ACHIEVING ONE
OF THE MOST OVERWHELMING DEFEATS OF FEDERAL
FORCES DURING THE ENTIRE WAR.

ERECTED BY THE STATE OF TEXAS 2009

Battle of Richmond, Kentucky

October 30, 1862

The Situation

From the outset of the Civil War, the leadership of the Confederacy recognized that to ultimately prevail in the conflict, it had only to defend its borders. Direct attacks against the much-stronger Union enemy would likely be less than prudent and probably disastrous. The audacious Gen. Robert E. Lee, once in command of the Army of Northern Virginia, saw things much differently. Not one to merely fend off his enemy's forces, Lee much preferred to take the war out of the Confederacy and into neutral states, or areas occupied by Yankee troops, and even onto Union soil. With Lee's victory at the Second Battle of Manassas, Confederate President Jefferson Davis seemed to share his truculent if elegant general's approach to offensive action, resulting in a sudden change in the South's strategy in the war.

That change was soon reflected both in Lee's invasion of Maryland in 1862 and in the Western Theater at the same time. In what seems to have been a broad government-coordinated plan of attack, Maj. Gen. Edmund Kirby Smith put his forces of the Department of Kentucky into motion to retake the Kentucky territory lost to the Union previously in the war. The goals of the overall offensive strategy were the same in the invasion of both Maryland and Kentucky. The starving Confederate Army would find either new or replenished sources of sustenance in the conquered countryside, the supposedly Southern-leaning citizenry in both states would hopefully offer new recruits for the Confederate Army, and, of course, the aggressive invasions might perhaps impress upon European leaders that the Confederacy was a strong and viable nation worthy of international recognition and support.

In 1862, Maj. Gen. Edmund Kirby Smith committed Confederate forces under his command to retake federally held positions in Kentucky, hoping Southern sympathizers in the area would rally to support the effort. *Courtesy of Library of Congress, LC-B813-2013 A, LOT 4213.*

Once General Kirby Smith's invaders were back in Kentucky, he and Gen. Braxton Bragg, his irascible fellow commander, issued separate proclamations that would, they hoped, prove to be reassuring to the citizens and promote their whole-hearted support of the Confederate cause. The two Kentucky proclamations were in many ways not dissimilar in content from the one General Lee had issued in his invasion of Maryland just a few days prior. In his message, Kirby Smith declared the Southern army had not come to Kentucky as invaders, while Bragg claimed that he had not led his army into the state as conquerors. Lee, in his proclamation, made it clear that no constraint upon the free will of Marylanders was intended by his invasion and that no intimidation of them would be allowed. The messages contained in these three documents clearly centered on a common theme, even though Lee's words were more eloquent and Kirby Smith and Bragg's were almost wheedling. No matter the style of each proclamation, the reaction to them was by and large the same: Few Kentuckians responded by joining the Confederate Army while Kirby Smith and Bragg were within their state, and not many Marylanders welcomed General Lee with anything more than cold indifference.

The Confederate invasion, known officially as the Kentucky Campaign, began on August 14, 1862. General Kirby Smith marched his ten thousand men out of Tennessee to unite with General Bragg's four divisions, which had come east by rail from Mississippi to participate in the invasion. The specific tactical goal of the invasion was to rid western Kentucky of Union troops that would make possible the eventual possession, first, of Lexington, and then, the state capital at Frankfort. If successful, the invasion might well persuade reluctant Kentuckians that their proper place in the Civil War was as a full-fledged Confederate state.

On August 29, 1862, General Kirby Smith's advance cavalry, commanded by Col. John Scott, encountered a small Union force a few miles south of Richmond, a small city some forty-five miles southeast of Frankfort. The Northern soldiers managed to halt the cavalrymen and push them back after a brief skirmish. The obvious willingness of the Union forces to resist his advance came as welcome news to General Kirby Smith because it indicated that his enemy would stand and fight in front of Richmond rather than at a much stronger natural defensive position located north of the town. As Scott's troopers rested following their short retreat, he received more than ample reinforcements commanded by Brig. Gen. Patrick Cleburne. Soon after Cleburne's arrival, what became the running Battle of Richmond began to unfold.

Maj. Gen. Edmund Kirby Smith, the victor of the Battle of Richmond, died in 1893 at the age of sixty-eight in Sewanee, Tennessee, where he was a mathematics professor at the University of the South. He was the last full general of the Confederate Army to die.

The Battle

On the morning of August 30, 1862, General Cleburne began moving back toward Richmond to confront the Union force of seven thousand troops commanded by Brig. Gen. Mahlon Manson. Most of Manson's men were green and untested in battle. Their commander, a onetime druggist, was also largely untested, having been in combat only twice before during the war.

Cleburne engaged Manson's Brigade in a two-hour attack that combined slow artillery barrages with infantry sorties that rendered the druggist-general's soldiers virtually powerless to resist such an organized advance. As Manson began withdrawing, a brigade commanded by Brig. Gen. Charles Croft, a former railroad president who had been a brigadier only since July 16, 1862, joined the forces. Although he had fought with Gen. Ulysses S. Grant at Fort Donelson and Shiloh, the new general was no match for such seasoned field commanders as Cleburne and Kirby Smith. Suspecting his two inexperienced brigadiers would be unlikely to resist Cleburne and Kirby Smith, Maj. Gen. William Nelson hurried to Richmond to assume overall command of the Union troops that were already reeling before the Confederate advance. Nelson, a veteran of the Mexican War, assembled his frightened soldiers, hoping to rally them by personally marching back and forth in front of the ranks claiming that if a Confederate

Maj. Gen. William Nelson, commander of all Union forces at Richmond, was the only onetime naval officer on either side to become a major general during the Civil War.

bullet could not hit him, none would hit them either. When it was painfully demonstrated that their general was not at all immune to enemy firepower, the Union men broke into a wild retreat to reach the presumed safety of the streets of Richmond. Unfortunately for the routed troops, Colonel Scott and his cavalrymen entered the little city from the rear while General Nelson indulged in his foolish display of bravery. Completely flummoxed by being attacked from both front and rear, more than 4,300 Union soldiers simply threw down their weapons in abject surrender.

During the battle, the North suffered serious casualties, including 206 killed and 844 wounded, as well as the huge number captured. General Croft was among those killed and General Manson was among those taken prisoner. General Cleburne received a slight wound in the fight. General Nelson survived his superficial wound and escaped, only to be shot to death one month later during a confrontation with a fellow Union general.

The Confederates captured not only the thousands of Union soldiers, but also an entire supply train, ten thousand small arms, and nine field pieces. It was an ignominious defeat for the North and, at least for a time, appeared to have had far reaching significance for the Confederacy. It lost only 78 men killed, with 372 wounded and one man reported missing in action. When the smoke cleared, it seemed the Confederate situation in Kentucky had been greatly improved by the total annihilation of Nelson's entire command.

On September 3, four days after his victory at Richmond, General Kirby Smith occupied Lexington and shortly thereafter moved on to Frankfort. With the capital city his, Kirby Smith and the Confederate government rejoiced in the perception that the South had regained Central Kentucky for good and that it now stood ready to take back other previously lost sections of the Western Theater as well. That perception, however, soon proved to be false.

The Texans

Among the Texas units participating in the Battle of Richmond were the following elements of Col. Thomas H. McCray's Brigade:

- 10th Texas (Dismounted) Cavalry Regiment
- 11thTexas (Dismounted) Cavalry Regiment
- 14th Texas (Dismounted) Cavalry Regiment
- 32nd [15th] Texas (Dismounted) Cavalry Regiment
- 1st Texas Artillery (Capt. James P. Douglas's Battery). It was Douglas's Battery that fired the first shots of General Cleburne's barrage on August 30, 1862.

All these units were part of Ector's Brigade, McCown's Division.

The Monument

The first state monument on the Richmond battlefield, the Texas monument is situated along a walking trail at a site overlooking Churchill's Draw, a strategic point where Texas forces served with distinction in the fighting. In partnership with the Battle of Richmond Association, and other groups, and with generous funding from various sources, including the Austin (TX) Civil War Round Table, the Texas Historical Commission (THC) formally dedicated the monument on Saturday, May 23, 2009. Although the ceremony went off without a hitch, there was some doubt about its success only a few days previously when

The current pastoral setting of the Richmond Battlefield in Kentucky belies the intense fighting that occurred here in late August 1862. Beyond the Texas monument, *center*, is the steep ravine known as Churchill's Draw, essential to the swift and decisive movement of Texas troops during the battle. *Photograph by Dan K. Utley.*

a crew from Austin's Stasswender Memorials, general contractors for fabricating and placing the stone, arrived on the battlefield. They were met with a continuing deluge of rain—accompanied by the threat of a tornado—that soaked the ground, causing their truck to get mired in mud. Rescued by tractor, the crew continued with the placement, despite "crane issues," and had the monument in place in time for the concrete to cure properly so it would not topple over during the dedication.

On the day of the dedication, a large crowd gathered under shade trees at the restored Pleasant View House (c. 1825), a battlefield landmark on the day of fighting in October 1862. Among those who joined in the dedication ceremony were hundreds of students participating in a battlefield cleanup and preservation project sponsored by the Civil War Trust and the History Channel. The program included the presentation of colors by the Madison County Marine Corps League and a talk titled "Texicans at Richmond" by Civil War historian and educator Douglas Lippman. Following his remarks, the Corps color guard led participants on a procession to the veiled monument some two hundred yards away. Students from a local middle school joined the procession carrying flags representing various regiments and states involved in the battle, with the Texas Lone Star flag in front. After THC military sites coordinator William McWhorter and Madison County Historic Properties director Phillip Seyfrit unveiled the monument, two young girls—Anna and Sarah Burns—

laid yellow roses at its base. A rifle squad then fired a twenty-one-gun salute and the program concluded with the playing of "Taps."

Texans Remember

Although Ector County is located in far West Texas—Odessa is the county seat—its namesake, Mathew Duncan Ector, is buried in far East Texas, in the Greenwood Cemetery at Marshall, Harrison County.

Directions to Monument

The monument is located in Battlefield Park off Battlefield Memorial Highway (US 421), south of Richmond. From the north end of the visitor center parking lot, a paved trail leads north, where it intersects with another paved trail to the left that leads to the Texas monument and the area of Churchill's Draw.

Suggested Readings

Brown, Kent Masterson, ed. *The Civil War in Kentucky: Battle for the Bluegrass State.* Mason City, IA: Savas Publishing, 2000.

Lambert, D. Warren. *When the Ripe Pears Fell: The Battle of Richmond, Kentucky.* Richmond: Madison County Historical Society, 1996.

TEXAS
REMEMBERS THE VALOR AND DEVOTION OF
HER SONS WHO SERVED AT SHARPSBURG
SEPTEMBER 16-17, 1862.

HERE IN THE CORNFIELD EARLY ON THE
MORNING OF SEPTEMBER 17 THE TEXAS
BRIGADE HELPED BLUNT THE ATTACK OF
ELEMENTS OF MANSFIELD'S UNION CORPS.
ALMOST ALONE DURING THIS POWERFUL
FEDERAL ONSLAUGHT THE TEXAS BRIGADE
SEALED A THREATENING GAP IN THE
CONFEDERATE LINE. IN SO DOING THE 1ST
TEXAS INFANTRY REGIMENT SUFFERED A
CASUALTY RATE OF 82.3 PERCENT, THE
GREATEST LOSS SUFFERED BY ANY INFANTRY
REGIMENT, NORTH OR SOUTH, DURING THE WAR.
OF APPROXIMATELY 850 MEN ENGAGED THE
TEXAS BRIGADE COUNTED OVER 550.

....

A MEMORIAL TO TEXANS
WHO SERVED THE CONFEDERACY

ERECTED BY THE STATE OF TEXAS 1964

Battle of Sharpsburg, Maryland

Also known as Battle of Antietam

September 16–17, 1862

The Situation

With Maj. Gen. George B. McClellan still reeling in retreat from his failed Peninsular Campaign, US President Abraham Lincoln put into motion a plan that would bring his other scattered forces located in Northern Virginia into one large consolidated Union Army. For the position of commander of the new Army of Virginia, he chose Maj. Gen. John Pope. Distantly connected by marriage to the family of Mary Todd Lincoln, Pope served with distinction in the Mexican War. In April 1862, during the Civil War, he further served admirably in a series of engagements under the always critical eye of Maj. Gen. Henry W. Halleck. Pope's first move as commander of the forty-five thousand-man army was to strike southward to gain control of a vital Virginia railroad. Before he could accomplish his objective, however, his own railroad system came under attack by a smaller enemy force commanded by Maj. Gen. Thomas J. (Stonewall) Jackson. To counter the attack, Pope reversed his army's course and marched northward back toward Washington, DC. His line of march in pursuing Jackson took him to within a few miles of Manassas, the site of the Union's crushing defeat in the first major battle of the Civil War. In his eagerness to find Jackson's force and destroy it, Pope blundered into a fierce clash with not only Jackson but also the full body of Gen. Robert E. Lee's

Army of Northern Virginia. The outcome was the Second Battle of Manassas, a sound defeat of Pope's army and the end of his days as a significant participant in the Civil War. He was dispatched to far-off Minnesota to fight the Sioux, and Lincoln once again promoted the chronically hesitant General McClellan to be the general-in-chief of all Union forces.

The triumphant Lee faced several options following his victory at Second Manassas. He thought it would be a fatal folly to attempt to overrun the formidable defensive positions then firmly in place at Washington, although the short distance from Manassas to the federal capital must have made the idea of a full-scale attack on it tempting. Lee also recognized that he could not long keep his fatigued and famished men in the Manassas area, depleted as it was of provisions or forage. He could, of course, always turn his command around to march back toward Richmond, but that might well be perceived as a retreat, albeit perhaps his safest course of action. The other option was to invade the North and bring the war to the land of his enemy. To be sure, it would be risky, bold, and daring in the extreme, but invade he did.

Crossing the Potomac River on September 4, 1862 at a point just thirty-five miles north of Washington, Lee's army of more than fifty thousand men moved into the state of Maryland. In addition to the sheer audacious appeal of the bold action, several rationalizations made the invasion particularly inviting. First, his troops would find more than ample provisions in the heretofore untrammeled richness of the Maryland countryside. Maryland was a slave state and, in Lee's view at least, the presence of his army within its borders might well convince it to secede from the Union and join other slave states already in the Confederacy. Then, he believed, it would be likely that the coveted recognition of the breakaway Southern nation by England and France might well be forthcoming. Finally, and perhaps uppermost in Lee's thoughts about the rewards implicit with the invasion, would be the transfer of the ruinous and deadly fighting away from the turf of his beloved Commonwealth of Virginia.

If Lee harbored any clinging doubts his invasion would fail, they faded amidst his optimistic belief that the people of Maryland would warmly welcome their fellow Southerners. This optimism quickly dissolved when the Marylanders greeted General Lee and his soldiers with icy indifference. No doubt disappointed, Lee nevertheless remained undeterred in his ultimate goal of marching across the state to reach the key Union railway center at Harrisburg, Pennsylvania. Control of that center would cut off the Union's ready access to the Western Theater and set the stage for a full-scale attack on Washington from the northwest.

To facilitate his plan, General Lee purposely ignored the fundamental rules of conventional warfare. He divided his force, sending Jackson to occupy Harper's Ferry to secure his supply lines while he continued his northward progress across Maryland toward his Pennsylvania target. The specific plans for dividing his army and then reuniting it after Harper's Ferry were detailed in a highly confidential document known as Special Order Number 191, delivered to only a select number of Lee's senior commanders in the field. What followed after the delivery of that key special order became one of the more intriguing stories of the Civil War.

President Abraham Lincoln and Gen. George B. McClellan confer on military strategies at Sharpsburg (Antietam), Maryland, 1862. *Courtesy of Library of Congress. LC-B817-7948.*

Each Confederate commander confirmed his receipt of the document, but in the fog of war an extra copy went undelivered, detained as a keepsake by a staff officer. Obviously not realizing that Lee's invasion plans would be placed in great peril should the secret order fall into enemy hands, the young officer found a convenient and more utilitarian use for the paper, using it as a protective wrapping for cigars he carried with him.

After leaving a Confederate encampment near Frederick, Maryland, the staff officer put the carefully wrapped cigars in a pocket of his uniform, out of which they later eventually fell to the ground. As Union luck would have it, two noncommissioned officers of the 27th Indiana were resting in an open field where they found the cigars with the important wrapping paper intact. Although it is difficult to accept that the tired Yankee soldiers would do anything other than casually discard the wrapping to light up their new found treasure, these two men handed the complete package over to their company commander, who instantly recognized the important and urgent information written on the wrapping paper. That the copy so quickly made its way up the chain of command is another unlikely aspect of the story of the lost order, but in a short time, literally everything General McClellan needed to know about Lee's tactical plans for the next four days was in his hands. No doubt incredulous at this all but unbelievable stroke of luck, the usually overly cautious Young Napoleon acted upon the windfall of vital information with uncharacteristic alacrity. He quickly sent his army of nearly eighty-five thousand to find Lee's still separated army at its newly revealed various locations to smash the invaders, division by division, and very likely end the war in the process.

> Reportedly, Confederate Maj. Gen. James Longstreet immediately recognized the importance of keeping the contents of Special Order Number 191 out of enemy hands. As a precaution, he memorized the words and then chewed the paper upon which they were written into tiny illegible bits.

In another unlikely twist to the tale, General Lee learned from a Confederate-friendly eavesdropping informant that all of his immediate plans were not only known to his opponents, but also that McClellan was already on the march to dramatically and forcibly counter those plans to the immense advantage of the Union Army. The scene was now set for the bloody Battle of Sharpsburg.

The Battle

Lee, knowing that McClellan was usually slow to react to any changing battle situation, moved his army to take up a naturally favorable defensive position. There would not likely be any time, however, to build breastworks and entrenchments to thwart the Union attack to come, although then at a site not of his choosing. McClellan performed as he had so often done before. Fearing the suspiciously found lost order might be the bait for a clever trap and, as always, imagining that Lee's actual force of 18,000 was more like 110,000, the Young Napoleon slowed his march to such a degree that Lee managed to reunite his army. With the return of Jackson from his successful taking of Harper's Ferry, Lee now had some 38,000 men to face McClellan's effective strength of around 75,000. Knowing he was outnumbered by a ratio of two to one, a more conservative general than Lee would likely have recrossed the Potomac and abandoned the invasion. Lee, however, was neither conservative nor timid. As a result, he did not hesitate to establish his lines behind Antietam Creek, close to Sharpsburg, Maryland, on September 16, 1862.

McClellan arrived at last, having dawdled away the extremely rare opportunity of catching Lee, the "Gray Fox," with his army split into small components. Further,

Lee had no relatively safe place to put his men in a position to fend off McClellan's much larger army. At the outset of the actual fighting, Antietam Creek separated the two dueling forces. Even though he had numerical superiority, McClellan saw fit to divide his own attacking force into smaller elements. His men then charged the Confederates on both the left and right, and then began to hammer away at the center, hopefully to cause its eventual collapse. The first Union attack came at dawn on the September 16, its initial success nullified by a powerful counterattack by Brig. Gen. John Bell Hood's Texas Brigade. This exchange gave way to another four-hour-long series of attacks and counterattacks that accomplished little for either side but caused a combined casualty loss of thirteen thousand.

A good deal of the Union's delay in sweeping the greatly outnumbered Confederates from the field was later attributed to the tunnel vision of Maj. Gen. Ambrose Burnside. Grasping the importance of getting his men across Antietam Creek, Burnside apparently believed the desired crossing could only be accomplished by storming across one particular stone bridge. Unaware the creek was shallow enough to allow his men to simply wade across to the other side, Burnside wasted precious hours futilely hurling his men over the bridge and into deadly volley after volley of Confederate bullets.

The stone bridge across which the Union Maj. Gen. Ambrose Burnside so uselessly ordered his men to cross in the face of fierce enemy fire still stands. In ironic tribute to the failure of the hapless general to realize his men could have easily waded across the river, it is now known as Burnside's Bridge.

The morning of the first day had been comparatively more successful for the Union. Now legendary clashes at the Dunker Church and at what became known as Bloody Lane ultimately swung to McClellan's advantage, but at a terrible price. The timely arrival of A. P. Hill's Division from their mopping up duties at Harper's Ferry caused McClellan to halt his attack as nighttime fell. Although their relative positions on the battlefield changed only moderately, the strength of the two opposing armies had altered significantly by the time the sun set. McClellan held in reserve over half of his men to overpower Lee on the second day. Lee, however, threw nearly all of his forces into the desperate fighting on the first day. As a result, his army shrank to less than half its initial strength.

On the next day, September 17, sunrise found the opponents staring across the bloodied field, each side waiting for the other to commence firing. During the night some of Lee's officers attempted to persuade their commander the losses were much too great to afford another day of such carnage. Lee, however, refused to withdraw, believing to do so would be to tarnish the already-storied reputation of his highly vaunted Army of Northern Virginia. After some additional bloody fighting, however, Lee finally led his battered command back across the Potomac and away from Northern soil. His adventure had been costly. He lost 31 percent of his men, suffering a casualty level estimated to range from 10,000 to 14,000. His opponent suffered losses of 12,400 in the battle, destined to be one of the bloodiest clashes of arms in the entire Civil War.

The dramatic modern setting of the Texas monument provides a historical perspective of what was at the time of the battle a cornfield where Brig. Gen. John Bell Hood's Texas Brigade suffered devastating losses. *Courtesy of Texas Historical Commission.*

When the smoke of the battle finally cleared, the Confederacy saw the outcome of the battle as a draw. McClellan, who had foolishly failed to pursue Lee across the Potomac, believed Sharpsburg to have been a clear and tremendous victory. Despite the Union general's boastful claims of overwhelming success, the more realistic President Lincoln saw that it was at least an improvement in the performance of his vexing commander. Although less than enthusiastic about McClellan's costly effort to drive Lee back to Virginia, and angry about his general's unwillingness to pursue his withdrawing opponent, Lincoln found a critical use for the alleged victory so highly touted in the newspapers. After much consideration, he saw in the perceived defeat of the Army of Northern Virginia an opportunity to issue his pivotal Emancipation Proclamation. By so doing, the Civil War instantly became a crusade to end slavery in the entire United States and no longer only a battle to preserve the Union. Lincoln's proclamation proved to be the turning point in the ultimate decision by England and France not to recognize the Confederate States of America, endorsements that would have been vital to the Southern cause. Without the support of the major powers in Europe, the Confederacy failed to achieve its long-sought international status.

The Texans

Among the Texans fighting at Sharpsburg were:
- 1st Texas Infantry, Lt. Col. P. A. Work commanding
- 4th Texas Infantry, Lt. Col. B. F. Carter commanding

- 5th Texas Infantry, Capt. Isaac Newton Moreland Turner commanding
- Col. W. T. Wofford was in command of the Texas Brigade as part of Hood's Division, Longstreet's Corps.

The Monument

When Texas officials began planning for a monument on the Sharpsburg battlefield in the early 1960s, only one other Southern state—Georgia—had a monument there. Spearheading the effort on behalf of Texas was a Houston attorney, bibliophile, and Civil War historian, Cooper K. Ragan. In cooperation with John T. Duncan, a history instructor at Texas A&M College, and Col. Harold B. Simpson, then a newly hired history instructor at Hill County Junior College, who would later gain prominence as a chronicler of Hood's Texas Brigade, he helped select the monument site and draft the inscription. With regard to the proper battle name for the text, Ragan noted in a 1963 letter to George W. Hill, director of the Texas State Historical Survey Commission (and thereby head of the Texas Civil War Centennial Commission), "I am strongly of the opinion that we should call it 'Sharpsburg'"—the name then long preferred by Southerners and historians of the Confederacy. And he added, "Also enclosed are two Kodak pictures of scenes at the Cornfield. The Park Service maintains several roads through the battlefield, but the land is still owned by private individuals. So many of the markers are placed on these interior roads where they can be easily read by the tourists." The general location of the monument echoed a previous recommendation by Robert L. Lagemann, acting park superintendent, who wrote Hill, noting, "Not only did the Texas regiments in Hood's Division literally plug a threatening gap in the Confederate line in the Cornfield during a crucial phase of the early morning action, but in so doing one of them sustained the highest casualty rate for an infantry regiment of the entire war."

In the months following, Texas officials worked with park staff and also the Maryland Civil War Centennial Commission to finalize plans for the dedication ceremony, scheduled for Veterans Day, November 11, 1964. In a letter to George W. Hill on October 9, Maryland commission director Park W. T. Loy listed his general ideas for the event, among which was item number 8: "Included in our local participants will be one of our prize winning High School Bands and a number of members of impersonating Civil War Military Units, both Union and Confederate." Loy also noted the event was of particular interest to his group because, "The Program will be the last one in which the Maryland Commission will have participated in prior to its ultimate discharge."

As a separate addendum to his letter, Loy wrote: "With further reference to your letter of October 2, should your Washington participants by any chance include a personality from the *White House*, that fact would be most gratifying. However, the consideration wholly on a confidential basis should such possibility materialize, we would be prepared to meet the situation both as to publicity and security—even on short notice." Such

A National Park Service employee uses air pressure to clean the Texas monument prior to repainting. Antietam National Battlefield. *Courtesy Texas Historical Commission.*

a suggestion was not lost on the Texas officials, but President Lyndon B. Johnson was unable to attend. As an article in the Hagerstown newspaper, *The Daily Mail*, on November 10, 1964, noted:

> When plans first were set rolling for dedication of the new Texas State Monument on the Antietam Battlefield, sponsors of the project were hopeful that the Lone Star State's most illustrious son would be on hand for the unveiling of the monument.
>
> They figured that, since he currently was living in a big white house just 60-some miles away from the battlefield, that he easily could arrange to be on hand for the ceremonies. What they didn't figure, of course, was that their favorite son would be so exhausted after his successful battle to renew his lease on that big white house that he'd be back on his ranch in Texas for an extended rest—interrupted daily by Cabinet-level proceedings.

Despite the lack of a president, the event went off as planned, commencing in the early afternoon of November 11 to opening music by the South Hagerstown High School Band. Among the dignitaries on hand were: George B. Hartzog, Jr., Director of the National Park Service; former Maryland governor W. Preston Lane, then vice-president of the Maryland Civil War Centennial Commission; and Miss Maryland, Donna McCauley. Mrs. John G. Bower, Jr., a great-great niece of Francis Scott Key, oversaw the raising of the US flag, and Sharon Keesecker, a member of the band, played "America, The Beautiful" on "an authentic Antietam Battle Fife." Ragan provided the keynote address, noting that a Maryland woman, Jane Long, was the "Mother of Texas," and later adding that the Civil War was "an example of what happens when the radicals take charge in a nation." He tempered the latter statement by concluding that the Civil War Centennial gave "a consciousness to the states of the war's history" and served as "an example of heroism for future generations to follow."

Texans Remember

On the courthouse square in Woodville, Tyler County, Texas, is an Official Texas Historical Marker for Lieutenant Colonel Work. A native of Cloverport, Kentucky, he moved with his family to Texas in the late 1830s and eventually established a plantation near Town Bluff in Tyler County. He represented the county to the 1861 Secession Convention but soon resigned to raise a local military company known as the Woodville Rifles, which became Company F, 1st Texas Infantry, Hood's Texas Brigade. He rose to the position of regimental commander at Gaines' Mill, Virginia, and led the 1st Texas at such battle sites as Second Manassas, Fredericksburg, and Gettysburg. It was at Sharpsburg, however, that his regiment suffered the monumental losses in the fierce fighting in the cornfield. Not long after his distinguished service at Gettysburg, and following an illness that prevented him from participating in the fighting at Chickamauga, Work resigned his commission and returned to Texas. After regaining his health, he resumed his military service in 1864, continuing on until war's end.

Following the Civil War, Work practiced law in Woodville and New Orleans, and later he operated the steamboat *Tom Parker*, plying the waters of the Neches River in East Texas. He died in 1911 and was buried in the Old Hardin Cemetery near Kountze, Hardin County.

Directions to Monument

From the visitor center at Antietam National Battlefield, Sharpsburg, drive north on Dunker Church Road, then turn right on The Cornfield Avenue. The monument is ahead on the right side of the road.

Suggested Readings

Gallagher, Gary W. *The Antietam Campaign*. Chapel Hill: University of North Carolina Press, 2007.

McPherson, James M. *Crossroads of Freedom: Antietam*. New York: Oxford University Press, 2002.

Spears, Stephen W. *Landscape Turned Red: The Battle of Antietam*. New Haven: Ticknor and Fields, 1983.

TEXAS

REMEMBERS THE VALOR AND DEVOTION OF ITS SONS
WHICH SERVED AT CORINTH AND ITS SURROUNDING
ENVIRONS DURING THE WESTERN CAMPAIGN OF 1862.

HERE, IN THE DAYS FOLLOWING THE RETREAT OF
SOUTHERN FORCES FROM THE BATTLEFIELD OF
SHILOH, TWO CONFEDERATE ARMIES COMBINED TO
DEFEND THE STRATEGIC RAILROAD CROSSING AT
CORINTH. TEXANS FROM 18 DIFFERENT UNITS
ASSISTED IN THE DEFENSE UNTIL, HEAVILY OUT-
NUMBERED, THE CONFEDERATES WERE COMPELLED
TO ABANDON THE CITY ON THE 30TH OF MAY.

IN MID-SEPT., THE CONFEDERATE ARMY OF THE
WEST UNDER MAJOR GENERAL STERLING PRICE
MANEUVERED TO PREVENT UNION REINFORCEMENTS
FROM LEAVING THE THEATER OF OPERATIONS.
ON SEPT. 19, THE BATTLE OF IUKA WAS FOUGHT 23
MILES TO THE EAST OF CORINTH. THERE TEXANS OF
LOUIS HEBERT'S BRIGADE MADE REPEATED CHARGES
ON THE UNION FORCES. THE FIGHTING WAS INCON-
CLUSIVE AND PRICE WAS ABLE TO EXTRICATE HIS
ARMY AND RENDEZVOUS WITH MAJOR GENERAL EARL
VAN DORN IN RIPLEY (MS) TO CARRY OUT A BOLD PLAN
TO DRIVE THE UNION ARMY FROM WEST TENNESSEE
BY FIRST ATTACKING THEIR GARRISON AT CORINTH.

HERE, THE BATTLE OF CORINTH, FOUGHT ON THE
3RD AND 4TH OF OCT., CULMINATED IN THREE CHARGES
AGAINST THIS SITE LED BY COL. WILLIAM P. ROGERS
OF THE 2ND TEXAS INFANTRY. THE ATTACKS FAILED
AND ROGERS WAS KILLED. TEXANS FROM BRIGADIER
GENERAL CHARLES PHIFER'S BRIGADE ADVANCED
SOUTHEAST BEYOND THIS POINT, BRIEFLY CAPTURING
THE RAILROAD CROSSROADS AT THE HEART OF THE
CITY, BEFORE COMPELLED TO RETIRE. VAN DORN'S
SHATTERED ARMY RETREATED WEST AND ON THE
FOLLOWING DAY, WHILE ATTEMPTING TO CROSS THE
HATCHIE RIVER AT DAVIS BRIDGE (TN), THE SONS OF
TEXAS WERE AGAIN CONSPICUOUS IN HOLDING BACK
ATTACKING UNION FORCES UNTIL A RIVER CROSSING
COULD BE SECURED UPSTREAM.

ERECTED BY THE STATE OF TEXAS 2010

Battle of Corinth, Mississippi

Also known as Second Battle of Corinth

October 3–4, 1862

The Situation

In early April 1862, Union Maj. Gen. Ulysses S. Grant ordered a massing of his troops at Pittsburg Landing on the Tennessee River. From that deepwater port, he planned to lead his large force south to attack the Confederacy's important rail center at Corinth, Mississippi, located a short twenty miles away. The general considered the small city to be the most important strategic location between the Tennessee and the Mississippi rivers. Confederate Gen. P. G. T. Beauregard, who would soon be called upon to defend the town, had previously claimed that to lose Corinth to the Union was to lose the whole Mississippi River and, perhaps, even the entire Southern cause.

The Confederates' surprise attack on General Grant's staging area at Pittsburg Landing led to what became known as the Battle of Shiloh. Even though that battle ended in a Union victory, Grant delayed his planned move toward Corinth and in the process damaged his own reputation through a widespread perception that his generalship during the fight had been for the most part unacceptable. Maj. Gen. Henry W. Halleck, Grant's immediate superior officer, took advantage of the public outcry over his lackluster performance to assume field command of the army still gathered at Pittsburg Landing. Never trustful of Grant anyway, and always eager to gain stature as a successful field commander, Halleck relegated Grant to a position as second in command after Shiloh, rendering him without a say in the still strategically important and long-planned attack on Corinth. Disgusted, Grant asked to be reassigned to another theater to free himself from Halleck's continuing disfavor. He also reportedly considered resigning his commission altogether, but his friend and fellow officer, William Tecumseh Sherman, persuaded him to abandon that idea.

On April 29, 1862, three weeks after Shiloh, Halleck moved out of Pittsburg Landing to resume Grant's original plan. At the beginning of the march, the new field commander had roughly ninety thousand men in his force. Fearing Confederates were likely to once again surprise and endanger his Corinth-bound army, Halleck insisted that each encampment along the route of march be heavily defended. He also ordered the construction of roads that proved costly in time and largely unnecessary. Given the caution and overbuilding that marked Halleck's march, it required a month to cover the twenty miles to Corinth. General Beauregard, who led his defeated army to Corinth following Shiloh, had under his command some sixty-six thousand troops either within the city or bivouacked on its outskirts. Knowing Corinth was Grant's original objective and now Halleck's, Beauregard ordered the construction of extensive lines of fortifications at the town and then patiently waited for what one historian described as Halleck's glacial advance to reach his works.

Lawrence Sullivan Ross commanded the 6th Texas Infantry during the Battle of Corinth. A veteran of 135 battles during the war, he later served two terms as governor of Texas. At the time of his death in 1898, he was president of what is today Texas A&M University.

As it developed, Beauregard's defenses were not to be tested for many months to come. When he learned Halleck had not only finally arrived on its outskirts but now also planned to level Corinth with a massive artillery barrage, Beauregard chose to save his army by simply abandoning the town. As the Union soldiers slept during the night of May 29, the large Confederate force silently slipped away under cover of darkness. The Corinth that Halleck thus took without a single shot being fired was by all accounts a sinkhole of pestilence. Reports indicate that as many Confederate soldiers had died of disease within the city as had died during the fighting at Shiloh.

Soon after he arrived at Corinth, General Halleck received orders to report to Washington, where he assumed the position of general-in-chief of all Union armies. His new position was not at all as glorious as the title might have indicated. Some commentators suggest that Halleck's tortoise-like advance on Corinth was not viewed at all favorably by President Lincoln and that as general-in-chief, Halleck was in fact relegated to what amounted to a role that was nothing more than that of a high-ranking clerk. At any rate, Halleck soon restored his nemesis, General Grant, back to field command in the West, clearing the way for that much-maligned general's legendary leadership in the balance of the war. The Union army, without Halleck, remained in Corinth, repairing and protecting the two key railroad lines that intersected in the city. The army was then under the command of Maj. Gen. William S. Rosecrans.

After leading his men safely out of Corinth to spare them the dire effects of Halleck's impending artillery bombardment, General Beauregard took ill and Gen. Braxton Bragg replaced him. Not one to stay on the defensive, the new army commander began his drive into Kentucky that later climaxed at the Battle of Perryville. To support his initial campaign in Kentucky. Bragg ordered Maj. Gen. Earl Van Dorn to move into Tennessee. To facilitate that move, Van Dorn thought it prudent to first attempt to reoccupy Corinth and its important railway systems, namely the Memphis & Charleston line, the key east-west route that intersected the Mobile & Ohio line, which in turn connected Kentucky with the Gulf of Mexico. In late September 1862, Van Dorn moved to attack Rosecrans at Corinth. Two weeks later, the two armies clashed in a short but significant battle at the city.

Confederate Maj. Gen. Earl Van Dorn, in command of Southern forces at the Battle of Corinth, died during the Civil War but not on the field. A cuckolded doctor who believed Van Dorn had "violated the sanctity of his home" assassinated the general at his headquarters in May 1863.

The Battle

During both the previous Confederate occupation and the later Union encampment, the small town of Corinth had been heavily fortified. Southern forces had built a chain of small field forts, or batteries, each surrounded by four to five hundred yards of felled timber. An enemy force would find it difficult to charge through the jumble of fallen tree trunks, all the while attempting to avoid the shells being fired at them from the batteries. The town itself was less than a mile behind the line of batteries and further protected by a second line of fortifications.

On the morning of October 3, Van Dorn's men hurled their way through the logs and toward the batteries. To make matters even more difficult for the attackers, three small earthquake tremors occurred just as the battle began, causing the Confederates to believe that much larger caliber cannon were being used against them. Rallied by Van Dorn, his command fought its way through to the second defensive line. According to a postbattle report written by the defending General Rosecrans, the midday temperature during the attack was higher than ninety degrees. The combination of heat and fatigue generated by making their way through the log barriers forced the Confederates to abruptly come to a halt, unable to push on. It took a full hour for Van Dorn and his officers to sufficiently admonish the weary troops to resume the attack. During the hour of rest, Union troops reinforced yet another line of defense that created even more difficult obstacles for the attackers. As darkness fell, Van Dorn halted the slowed advance and the fighting stopped for the night.

Early the next morning, Confederate artillery began a bombardment of the Union batteries. The barrage triggered an answering fire that briefly halted a second attempt to breach all Union lines of defense to take back the city. The Confederate attack failed when two of Van Dorn's brigadiers, Mansfield Lovell and Louis Hébert, failed to maneuver as ordered. Hébert was ill and therefore replaced by an officer who hesitated before attacking. At Battery Robinett, Confederate Col. William P. Rogers died while leading his 2nd Texas Infantry over its ramparts. Rogers's bravery in the face of point-blank fire earned him the posthumous admiration of troops on both sides of the conflict.

Early in the afternoon of October 4, Van Dorn recognized the futility of hurling his still exhausted and thirsty men against the clearly impenetrable Union defense. He halted the

Col. William P. Rogers, killed while boldly advancing the colors of the 2nd Texas Infantry at Battery Robinett, was a medical doctor who later served as a law professor at Baylor University before the war. Governor Sam Houston was among his legal clients. Following the fighting at Corinth, Rogers was buried with full military honors during a ceremony ordered by Union Maj. Gen. William S. Rosecrans.

troops, led them out of the battle in a westerly direction, and escaped the tepid pursuit only half-heartedly launched by Rosecrans. When the two brigades sent to the battlefield by General Grant arrived too late to pursue and overtake the fleeing Confederates, the Battle of Corinth came to its end. It had been a costly fight for both sides. Union casualties were reported to be 2,520 killed or wounded out of 21,247 effectives, whereas the Confederates losses were estimated to be 2,470 killed or wounded and 1,763 missing in action out of some 22,000 combatants. Union general Pleasant Adam Hackleman was among the men killed in the fighting.

The Texans

Among the many Texas units at Corinth were:
- 2nd Texas Infantry
- 6th Texas Infantry
- 9th Texas Infantry
- Good's Battery
- Teel's Battery
- 1st Texas Dismounted Cavalry
- 3rd Texas Dismounted Cavalry
- 6th Texas Dismounted Cavalry
- 9th Texas Dismounted Cavalry
- 10th Texas Dismounted Cavalry
- 11th Texas Dismounted Cavalry
- 15th Texas Dismounted Cavalry
- 16th Texas Dismounted Cavalry
- 17th Texas Dismounted Cavalry
- 27th Texas Dismounted Cavalry
- 32nd Texas Dismounted Cavalry
- Wharton's Texas Rangers

The Monument

The Texas monument at Corinth represents not only valor and military strategy, but also, on another less evident level, the role of compromise in commemorative interpretation. When the Corinth battle sites officially became part of the Shiloh National Military Park in 2000, prevailing park policy regarding monumentation was that an adherence to the historic landscape should prevail. Although that did not preclude signs, markers, and monuments entirely, it limited their presence significantly. Plans for a Texas monument, among others, began even as the National Park Service (NPS) worked to complete a site plan that would guide future questions about seventeen individual sites related to the siege, battle, and

National Park Service rangers carefully drape the Texas monument at Corinth prior to its formal unveiling in 2010. *Courtesy of Texas Historical Commission; William A. McWhorter, photographer.*

subsequent occupation of Corinth. Working in partnership, the Texas Historical Commission (THC) and the Siege and Battle of Corinth Commission pressed federal officials for an exemption to park policy that would allow for a Texas monument. Rosemary T. Williams, chair of the Corinth commission, worked with Mississippi Senator Trent Lott, and others, for that purpose. The process proved lengthy, but in September 2008, NPS Director Mary A. Bomar notified THC Chairman John L. Nau, III, that "pursuant to the Act of December 27, 1894, as amended . . . which establishes Shiloh National Military Park and the Corinth Unit of this park and requires approval of the design, inscriptions and placement of monuments in this park, and consistent with National Park Service regulations . . . for installation of commemorative works . . . the monument to commemorate the Texas troops as proposed by the Texas Historical Commission and described and depicted in the attachments to your letter, is approved." Final planning for the monument got underway immediately thereafter, and on October 3, 2010, Nau presented the keynote address at the dedication ceremony for the Texas monument at Corinth, significantly sited in the vicinity of Battery Robinett.

Texans Remember

On the north side of the courthouse square in San Saba, Texas, is an Official Texas Historical Marker commemorating the United Confederate Veterans (UCV) William P. Rogers Camp

No. 322. The UCV began in 1889 to honor Confederate veterans, both living and dead, and the San Saba camp, named for the hero of Corinth, Colonel Rogers, formed four years later. Although Rogers never lived in San Saba County, his daughter, Fannie Alabama Rogers Harris, did. Fannie and her husband, George Harris, moved to the county in 1880, and upon formation of the UCV camp, he served as the first commander. The local group remained active in its early years through educational programs and annual meetings, but a decline in veterans by the 1930s caused the camp to disband.

At Old Settlers' Park in Round Rock in Central Texas, a state marker honors two brothers, Edward and John Hudson, who both served as Confederate chaplains during the Civil War. Wounded in battle as a soldier at Corinth, Edward nevertheless became a chaplain there, replacing another chaplain killed in action. Later in Georgia, Edward was again wounded, this time critically, but he survived and returned to Texas, where he preached in various counties until his death in 1877. John, like his brother, a Presbyterian, served as a soldier with the 19th Texas Cavalry before his commission as a chaplain in March 1863. He, too, returned to Texas following the war and continued to preach. He died in 1914. The two veterans, believed to be the only brothers who served as chaplains in the war, are buried in the Round Rock Cemetery.

Directions to Monument

Corinth Battlefield Interpretive Center, 501 W. Linden Street, Corinth.

Suggested Readings

Cozzens, Peter. *The Darkest Days of the War: The Battles of Iuka and Corinth*. Chapel Hill: University of North Carolina Press, 1997.

Dossman, Steven Nathaniel. *Campaign for Corinth: Blood in Mississippi*. Abilene, TX: McWhiney Foundation Press, 2006.

Smith, Timothy B. *Corinth 1862: Siege, Battle, Occupation*. Lawrence: University Press of Kansas, 2012.

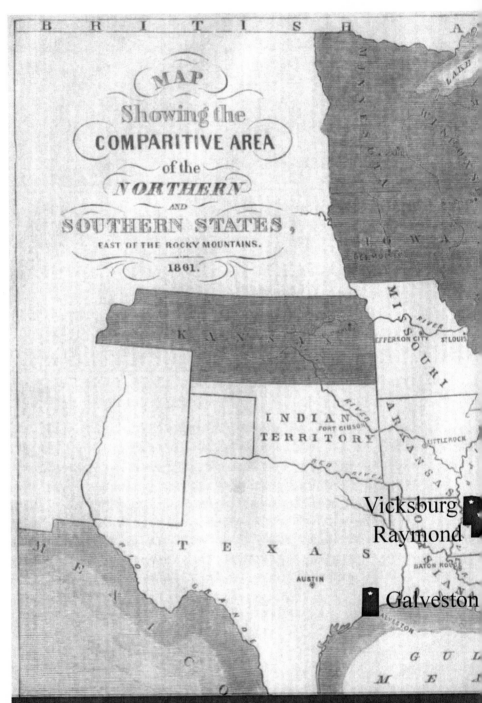

MAP
Showing the
COMPARITIVE AREA
of the
NORTHERN
AND
SOUTHERN STATES,
EAST OF THE ROCKY MOUNTAINS.
1861.

Vicksburg
Raymond
Galveston

Gettysburg was the price the South paid for having R. E. Lee.
—*Shelby Foote*

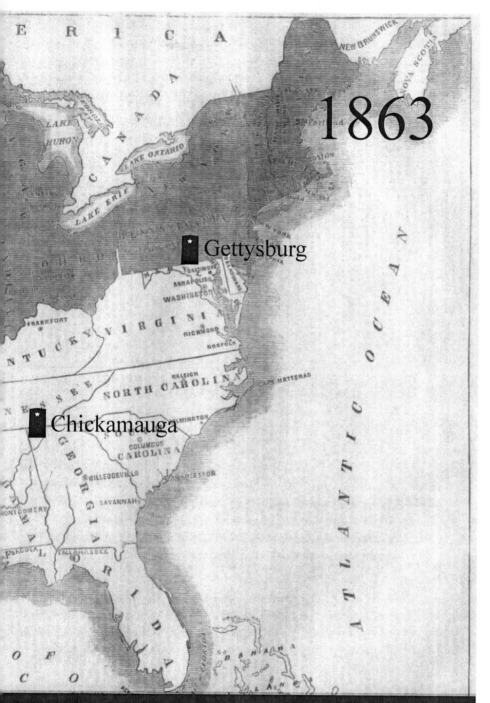

1863

Gettysburg

Chickamauga

Vicksburg, and not Gettysburg, was the crisis of the Confederacy.
—*J. F. C. Fuller*

TEXAS

REMEMBERS THE VALOR AND DEVOTION OF
THE MILITARY COMBATANTS AND CIVILIAN
INHABITANTS OF GALVESTON
DURING THE CIVIL WAR.

ON OCT. 9, 1862, A UNION NAVAL FORCE
LANDED AT GALVESTON AND RAISED THE U.S.
FLAG AT THIS CUSTOMHOUSE. BUT ON JAN. 1,
1863, IN THE BATTLE OF GALVESTON,
CONFEDERATE UNITS UNDER MAJ. GEN. J.B.
MAGRUDER RECAPTURED THE CITY, UTILIZING
ONLY FIELD ARTILLERY AND TWO STEAMBOATS
PROTECTED WITH COTTON BALES TO DEFEAT
UNION GUNBOATS AND A SMALL INFANTRY
FORCE. ON BOARD THE "COTTONCLAD"
STEAMBOATS, UNDER COMMAND OF MAJ. LEON
SMITH, WERE VOLUNTEERS LED BY COL.
THOMAS GREEN.
THIS CITY AND ITS RESIDENTS WERE
CONTINUALLY UNDER THE GUNS OF ONE SIDE
OR THE OTHER, AND OCCASIONALLY BOTH.
FROM THE START OF A UNION BLOCKADE IN
JULY 1861 UNTIL JUNE 2, 1865, WHEN THE
CONFEDERATE ARMY OF THE TRANS-
MISSISSIPPI SURRENDERED AT GALVESTON. FOR
THE CIVILIANS WHO REMAINED, LIFE IN A CITY
THAT WAS ESSENTIALLY AN ARMED CAMP
WAS DIFFICULT AND DANGEROUS.
ON JUNE 5, 1865, IN WHAT CAPT. BENJAMIN
SANDS OF THE U.S. NAVY CALLED THE
"CLOSING ACT OF THE GREAT REBELLION," HIS
FORCES AGAIN RAISED THE U.S. FLAG HERE,
FINALLY BRINGING UNDER UNION CONTROL
THE LAST MAJOR PORT STILL IN CONFEDERATE
HANDS. ON JUNE 19, 1865, UNION GEN. GORDON
GRANGER ISSUED AN ORDER IN GALVESTON
STATING THE EMANCIPATION PROCLAMATION
WAS IN EFFECT IN TEXAS. THAT EVENT, LATER
CELEBRATED AS "JUNETEENTH," CONFIRMED
THE END OF SLAVERY IN THE STATE.
A MEMORIAL NOT ONLY TO TEXANS WHO
SERVED IN THE MILITARY, BUT ALSO TO
THOSE WHO ENDURED HARDSHIPS AT HOME.

ERECTED BY THE STATE OF TEXAS 1998

Galveston, Texas

Monument is for the home front and for the Battle of Galveston

January 1, 1863

The Situation

Even as Texans prepared for the inevitability of secession, despite opposition by Gov. Sam Houston and others, state military forces moved on San Antonio and secured the surrender of Union forces under Gen. David E. Twiggs. The control seemingly evidenced by that action proved to be tenuous at best because Texas remained particularly vulnerable to attack along its sparsely settled western frontier, from the Indian Territory to the north, and especially along its expansive coastline. Additionally, Texas had to deal with Indian unrest, political instability in Mexico, a vexing federal blockade, and an influx of refugees from war-ravaged areas to the east. Uneasiness and uncertainty were pervasive throughout the state, and home guard units remained ever-vigilant as other forces joined up with the Confederacy to participate in battles from New Mexico to Pennsylvania. There were also Texas troops, however, who served in the Union Army.

Just as Vicksburg was the key to Union plans along the Mississippi valley, so too was the port city of Galveston in relation to control of Texas. Galveston was not only a vital seaport and the state's largest city, but it also had rail connections that could move Union forces into the interior quickly to disrupt lucrative cotton trade routes to Mexico and to isolate the state from the rest of the Confederacy. Despite its strategic value to the South, though, the island city of Galveston was particularly vulnerable—some would even say indefensible. That

John Bankhead Magruder, commander of Confederate forces during the Battle of Galveston. *Courtesy of Library of Congress. LC-USZ62-62496, Lot 4213.*

was clearly evident on October 4, 1862, when the federal gunboat *Harriet Lane* entered Galveston harbor and federal forces secured a surrender agreement, allowing time for the evacuation of women and children. Confederate troops remained in the vicinity, however, holding key points just outside the main part of the city. With the port in Union control, the rebels moved to secure the rail lines that would surely be the targets of pending attacks. As they did, three companies of the US 42nd Infantry under Col. Isaac Burrell landed at Galveston on Christmas day and took up a key position at Kuhn's Wharf along 18th Street. Their mission was to control the situation as best they could while awaiting the arrival of a much larger assault force.

Just prior to this point, Confederate leaders had turned to one of its most unlikely and controversial leaders, Maj. Gen. John Bankhead Magruder. Known as "Prince John" for his flamboyant manners and proclivities, the Virginia native had shown great military promise during the Mexican War and in the early days of the Civil War but seemingly squandered his reputation in a disappointing performance during the fight at Malvern Hill in the Peninsular Campaign. Regardless, he took control of the defensive planning for Texas, with his first key test at Galveston. His plan for recapturing the island city was to strike fast before Union reinforcements arrived, but he faced a considerable gap between tactics and reality, given the lack of weaponry and field personnel. His only relevant asset, it seemed, was the element of surprise, and so he prepared to attack from both land and water, with diversionary actions by infantry and artillery. Magruder's plan would involve high degrees of coordination and communication to be successful, but as it played out against a backdrop of battle there would be no doubt that luck and the inconsistencies of the human element also played significant roles in the outcome.

The Battle

For the naval operations, Magruder called on Commodore Leon Smith, a prior acquaintance. At Magruder's direction, Smith outfitted two gunboats—the *Bayou City* and the *Neptune*—with armor of readily available cotton bales. The so-called "cottonclads" carried both field artillery pieces and infantry sharpshooters, the latter under the command of Col. Tom Green, a veteran of Brig. Gen. Henry Hopkins Sibley's ill-fated 1862 expedition to New Mexico. On land, Magruder planned to open the battle with heavy artillery barrages from a position called Virginia Point and then to follow quickly with the use of flying artillery maneuvers within the city, as well as an infantry assault on Kuhn's Wharf using scaling ladders to thwart Union defenses via the water's edge.

Although Magruder hoped to begin his assault soon after Christmas, delays with the work on the cottonclads delayed action until the early morning hours of New Year's Day, 1863. With a flair for the dramatic, Magruder personally fired the signal shot that set all the components of battle into action. What followed was, in effect, a large staged action that featured the deafening roar of artillery from various points and the blurred frenzy of charging infantrymen, with gunboats poised nearby for their delayed entry.

The early morning surprise attack had the desired effect, causing considerable confusion among the Union forces, both naval and infantry. The USS *Westfield* moved from a position near Point Bolivar to the east in an effort to secure access to the bay but ran aground in the process. At Kuhn's Wharf, Burrell prepared his men for a frontal assault from the city, only to find the true vulnerability came from underneath the position. Confederates under Col. Joseph J. Cook moved quickly to the water's edge with cover support from sharpshooters, only to find their scaling ladders were insufficient in length to reach the top of the wharf. They quickly fell back under heavy Union fire from above. Through the confusing battle scene then came the cottonclads, bearing down quickly on the *Harriet Lane*, and for a time careful strategic planning seemed to give way to happenstance and the serendipity of battle amid close order ship-to-ship fighting and the relentless assault of boarding parties. Support from the USS *Owasco* failed to materialize under the withering fire, and the Confederates quickly gained the upper hand. Soon a white flag flew from the *Harriet Lane*. Union leaders on the scene counseled under a temporary truce and after assessing the damage and likelihood of success, opted for surrender. Isolated and without any means of reinforcement for his position, Burrell surrendered as well. The action, however, had not yet run its course.

As the Union ships prepared for an eventual break to the open sea, Commander William B. Renshaw moved to scuttle the foundering

Of the three US gunboats that managed to evade capture at Galveston under flags of truce, two—the *Sachem* and the *Clifton*—would not escape in the later Battle of Sabine Pass farther east along the Texas coast. The third, the *Owasco*, provided limited support in preparation for the assault on Fort Griffin at Sabine Pass, but her captain eventually raised the US flag at the site at the close of the war in May 1865.

This wood engraving depicts the deadly explosion that destroyed the USS *Westfield* on January 1, 1863, at Galveston. *Courtesy of Library of Congress, LC-USZ62-74022.*

Westfield. Although the exact details of the events that followed are conjectural, the results proved to be the same—the magazines of the Union flagship prematurely ignited, causing a massive explosion that killed the commander and his party of crew members. With that, the three Union gunships still viable and not under Confederate control—the *Clifton, Owasco,* and *Sachem*—made safe their escape to open water under flags of truce and with the CSS *John F. Carr* in pursuit. As the escaping ships crossed the bar, the Battle of Galveston came to an end six hours after the opening shot, and the port city was again in Confederate control. Peace for the beleaguered city was tenuous at best, though, as Union ships continued to ply the coastal waters for the duration of the war. Another attack, however, never came, and at war's end, Galveston was the largest port city still in Confederate control. Its role in the conflict came to an end when officials of the Trans-Mississippi Department, CSA, signed surrender documents aboard the USS *Fort Jackson* just off shore on June 2, 1865. Seventeen days later, on June 19, Union Brig. Gen. Gordon Granger announced in Galveston that President Abraham Lincoln's Emancipation Proclamation was in effect, formally ending the institution of slavery in Texas. Through the years, that date became known as Juneteenth and is now celebrated and recognized worldwide by diverse cultures as a landmark day of freedom.

The Texans

Participants in the Battle of Galveston included elements of the following:

- Cook's Regiment of the 1st Texas Heavy Artillery
- Elmore's 20th Texas Infantry
- 4th Texas Cavalry
- 5th Texas Cavalry
- 7th Texas Cavalry
- Debray's 26th Texas Cavalry
- Pyron's 2nd Texas Mounted Rifles
- Griffin's 21st Cavalry Battalion
- Texas State Militia
- Engineer Corps
- Martin's 10th Texas Cavalry Battalion
- Daly's Company of Cavalry

Texas Marine Department, including the ships:

- *Bayou City*
- *Neptune*
- *John F. Carr*
- *Lucy Gwinn*
- *Royal Yacht*

The Monument

The Galveston Civil War Monument is significant because it commemorates not only a battle but the home front as well. It also honors Juneteenth—June 19—Emancipation Day in Texas. In many ways, too, the Galveston monument represents a transition of public commemoration dealing with the Civil War. The state's first monument placed beyond the initial scope of the Texas Civil War Centennial Commission, it reflects the modern era of wartime remembrance, with broader perspectives that speak to the cultural and social impacts of armed conflict, as well as the educational value of monument texts.

Determining an appropriate place for the Texas monument proved particularly difficult, as much of the original battle scene and antebellum harbor area have given way to industrial development and shoreline reclamation. Kuhn's Wharf, a pivotal point in the fighting, for example, has long since disappeared. One of the few extant remnants of the battle is the nearby Hendley Building (Hendley's Row) at 2016 Strand, where General Magruder fired the signal shot that set his attack into motion. In the end, all sponsoring parties for the monument agreed on property adjacent to the 1859 US Customs House at 20th and Post Office streets. During the 1865 battle, the Customs House was a key landmark, with troops using it for cover as they made their assaults

John L. Nau, III, chairman of the Texas Historical Commission, and Betty Massey, director of the Galveston Historical Foundation, unveil the Galveston monument, 1998. The monument was the first placed since the efforts of the Texas Civil War Centennial Commission in the 1960s and represented a new era of battlefield interpretation. *Courtesy of Texas Historical Commission.*

or regrouped following the near disaster at the wharf. As a federal installation, it was also an important symbol of continuity and stability in the days of Reconstruction that followed the war.

Despite the reconfiguration of the historic landscape through the years, Galveston is a city that prides itself on historic preservation and heritage tourism. As a result, city officials and members of the Galveston Historical Foundation (GHF) and the Galveston County Historical Commission worked closely with the Texas Historical Commission (THC) to secure funding for the project and to develop a monument text that was accurate, inclusive, and educational. Following those guiding principles, the GHF sponsored a historical conference to coincide with the monument dedication on January 2, 1998. The conference included an exhibit opening and reception that evening at the Galveston County Historical Museum, and attendees of the special Civil War Weekend participated in tours (both by land and by sea), viewed artifacts and document collections, heard presentations by some of the state's most noted Civil War historians, and joined in a cemetery memorial honoring both Union and Confederate veterans.

During the Civil War, the 1850s Greek Revival structure known as Hendley's Row had a rooftop cupola used as a lookout post for both Union and Confederate troops.

Preparation for the Galveston monument showed a great deal had changed in the three decades since the State of Texas initiated the commemorative program in the 1960s. For one thing, the price of the monolithic pink granite stone had risen in cost from $750 to more than $10,000. There was also an increase in the amount of text, with more emphasis on the educational value of public history. And too, there were some differences of opinion among potential sponsors, including a lengthy debate over whether the name of the conflict should be the Civil War (the state's position) or the War Between the States (the position of several key donors). In the end, the state prevailed and the private funding came through as promised, but such seemingly minor disputes revealed that emotions about the war still run deep.

At the dedication ceremony, historian Edward T. Cotham, Jr., of Houston, provided the keynote remarks he titled "Galveston in the 1860s." Then, befitting his role as the architect of the newly revised Texas in the Civil War Monument program, THC chairman John L. Nau, III, joined with GHF executive director Betty Massey in unveiling the monument. Under Nau's direction, other THC monuments would follow at places like Raymond and Corinth in Mississippi and Richmond and Rowlett's Station in Kentucky, but the one at Galveston served as the model for the modern era.

Texans Remember

Of the many historical markers that reference Galveston during the Civil War, perhaps the most compelling is one at the gravesite of Lt. Cdr. Edward Lea in the Trinity Episcopal Cemetery (lot 5, section 18) at Broadway and 40th in Galveston. The Maryland-born Lea grew up in a military family; his father, Albert, was a West Point graduate and a native of Tennessee. At the onset of the war, both men chose to participate in the fighting, albeit on opposite sides. Albert opted to join with the Confederacy, whereas his son, a promising US naval officer, remained in Union service. As the fates would have it, both appeared on the scene in the Battle of Galveston—Albert on the staff of General Magruder and Edward as First Officer of the ill-fated *Harriet Lane*. Following the battle, Edward frantically searched for his son, eventually finding him in grave condition with multiple gunshot wounds. In his dying moments, there with his father, Edward lovingly inquired about his family members. Following this brief exchange, Albert left to secure medical attention for his son. In his absence, those attending the young naval officers—both his shipmates and Confederate soldiers—asked if they could help ease his suffering, but he declined, adding with his final words, "My father is here."

The following day, Magruder approved a funeral service attended by both victors and prisoners for Edward Lea and his commanding officer, Jonathan Wainwright. According to historian Cotham, "The two men were buried together in the same grave. . . . [And] Albert Lea read the funeral service over his son's remains, closing with these words: 'Allow one so sorely tried in this his willing sacrifice to beseech you to believe that while we defend our rights with our strong arms and honest hearts, those we meet in battle may also have hearts as brave and honest as our own. We have buried two brave and honest gentlemen. Peace to their ashes; tread lightly over their graves.'"

Directions to Monument
On Post Office Street east of the intersection with 20th Street on the grounds of the historic US Customs House, Galveston.

Suggested Readings
Cotham, Edward T., Jr. *Battle on the Bay: The Civil War Struggle for Galveston*. Austin: University of Texas Press, 1998.

Frazier, Donald S. *Cottonclads! The Battle of Galveston and the Defense of the Texas Coast*. Abilene, TX: McWhiney Foundation Press, 1998.

TEXAS

REMEMBERS THE VALOR AND DEVOTION OF
ITS SONS WHO PARTICIPATED IN THE
BATTLE OF RAYMOND AND IN OTHER
ENGAGEMENTS OF THE VICKSBURG CAMPAIGN.

UPON THIS FIELD ON MAY 12, 1863, SOLDIERS
OF THE 7TH TEXAS INFANTRY OF BRIGADIER
GENERAL JOHN GREGG'S BRIGADE, LED BY
REGIMENTAL COMMANDER COLONEL HIRAM B. GRANBURY,
FOUGHT WITH GRIM DETERMINATION AGAINST TWO
DIVISIONS OF FEDERAL FORCES UNDER THE COMMAND
OF MAJOR GENERAL JAMES B. McPHERSON.
THE UNION ADVANCE WAS PART OF A LARGER
CAMPAIGN DESIGNED TO CAPTURE THE STRATEGIC PORT
CITY OF VICKSBURG ON THE MISSISSIPPI RIVER.
LEADING THE CONFEDERATE ASSAULT AGAINST THE
FEDERALS, GRANBURY'S TEXANS STEPPED FORWARD
AT NOON AND SURGED ACROSS THE FOURTEEN MILE CREEK,
WHERE THEY MET THE ENEMY IN FORCE.
THEY VALIANTLY STRUGGLED WITH REGIMENTS
FROM OHIO AND ILLINOIS, WHILE ALL ALONG THE
BATTLE LINE THE SOUTHERN SOLDIERS OF GREGG'S
BRIGADE FACED THREE TIMES THEIR NUMBER.
DESPITE THEIR COURAGEOUS EFFORT, THE
CONFEDERATE TROOPS WERE CHECKED AND
FORCED FROM THE FIELD AROUND 4:30 P.M.
THE ENGAGEMENT AT RAYMOND WAS A PRECURSOR
TO THE INTENSE FIGHTING TO FOLLOW
DURING THE SIEGE OF VICKSBURG.

IN THE BATTLE OF RAYMOND, THE TEXANS LOST
22 MEN KILLED, 73 WOUNDED, AND 63 MISSING IN ACTION.

A MEMORIAL TO TEXANS WHO SERVED THE CONFEDERACY.

ERECTED BY THE STATE OF TEXAS 2001

Battle of Raymond, Mississippi

And the Vicksburg Campaign

May 12, 1863

The Situation

Confederate Gen. P. G. T. Beauregard had once warned that if the city of Corinth was lost to Union forces, the Southern cause might in time be lost as well. When the city finally fell to federal forces, Gen. William Tecumseh Sherman claimed after the war that the victory indeed enabled the Union to launch a broad offensive that would gain complete control of the Mississippi River for the United States. Both generals were correct. The offensive plan that would in the long run bring about the defeat of the Confederacy had as its objective the South's mighty military citadel of Vicksburg. Massively fortified, the site overlooked the Mississippi River from atop steep bluffs that afforded Confederate artillery the advantageous opportunity to destroy all enemy shipping that dared to attempt passing below its ramparts.

It had been a plan to conquer Vicksburg that brought Maj. Gen. Ulysses S. Grant to Pittsburg Landing in early April 1862. Massing his forces there, Grant intended to move rapidly southward to take Corinth and from there launch his assault on Vicksburg. The unexpected battle at Shiloh had delayed Grant's plan at great cost, but the Union would not be denied its long-desired occupation of Corinth. After thwarting a nearly successful recapture of Corinth by Confederate forces in October 1862, General Grant was at last able to undertake the vital assault on Vicksburg itself.

There was more to the citadel than just its formidable military prowess. Supplies from the Confederacy's Trans-Mississippi area flowed into Vicksburg en route to Southern cities in the East. Goods being transported on the river then went out to the entire Confederacy by rail from Vicksburg. No matter the cost, Grant believed the fortress had to be overcome. Conquering that fortress proved to be a particularly difficult task. Surrounded by twisting streams, deep bayous, and impenetrable swamps on its northern approaches and protected by the well-defended river on its west, Vicksburg would not be as readily taken as General Grant had hoped.

A series of early attempts by Grant's chief lieutenant, General Sherman, in December 1862 proved to be both costly and futile. Realizing the stronghold could only be taken by an assault from the south or east, Grant determined to abandon the attacks from the north and seek a more promising approach from another direction. His solution to the problem was unconventional but highly successful. On April 16 and April 22, 1863, Grant ordered the Union's naval flotilla located on the Mississippi River north of Vicksburg to run the gauntlet under the guns of the fortress to sail south past the expected barrage under the cover of night. Although enemy fire sank two of the boats in the process, Grant at last had the means to carry out his unique plan of attack. Marching his forty-three thousand-man army down the west banks of the river, Grant halted at the small town of Hard Times Landing, Louisiana. There his troops boarded the ships that had made it past the guns of Vicksburg and they sailed across the Mississippi to land on the opposite shore some thirty miles south.

Initially, the intended riparian assault was planned to take place at the Mississippi city of Grand Gulf, but Confederate artillery repulsed the Union gunboats sent ahead of the troop transports. Grant, undeterred, simply moved the landing point farther south. On April 30, his entire army came ashore at Bruinsburg, Mississippi. To divert attention from his initial march down the river's western bank, Grant ordered several diversionary maneuvers. While Sherman feinted with a sizeable force north of Vicksburg, Col. Benjamin Grierson's 6th Illinois Cavalry, 1,700 riders strong, distracted the Confederates with a six hundred-mile sweep east of the city, destroying communication lines and tearing up the tracks of southern railways in the process.

The day after his successful crossing of the river, Grant moved toward the well-defended city of Port Gibson. In a clash outside the town, a greatly outnumbered Confederate force briefly slowed Grant's men but soon gave way, suffering fewer than eight hundred casualties. The taking of Port Gibson in turn caused the key fortification at Grand Gulf to also surrender. Grant now weighed his options, and ultimately the route he chose to take brought the war directly to the people of Raymond, caught in the gun sights between the strategic points of Jackson to the east and Vicksburg to the west.

The Battle

The small town of Raymond lay in the path of General Grant's advance into western Mississippi, with the ultimate objective being the Mississippi River port city of Vicksburg.

The battle that took place at Raymond was of short duration, lasting a little more than six hours. Brig. Gen. John Gregg commanded the garrison defending the town, and Maj. Gen. James B. McPherson led the Union attacking force of twelve thousand troops. The skirmish took place less than four miles southwest of the town. Confederate artillery slowed the advance in a firefight that began in the open and then shifted into a heavily wooded area. The terrain made it difficult to identify who was an enemy and who was a friend. For several hours, it was a confused and dusty scene with neither side able to claim a clear victory.

When it became apparent to Gregg that he was not engaging a raiding party, as he initially believed, but perhaps a full brigade or more, he realized his highly outnumbered defenders could not prevail. Consequently, he broke off the fighting and withdrew through the town and on toward the state capital city of Jackson. McPherson's men did not pursue the retreating Confederates, although they moved into Raymond to bivouac for the night. The casualties were low on both sides, at least compared to many other similar shorter skirmishes. Union losses—killed, wounded, and missing—were reported to be less than five hundred, whereas Confederate losses—killed, wounded, and captured—ran slightly more than eight hundred.

> The Texas Secession Convention named John Gregg as one of six representatives to the provisional Confederate Congress at Montgomery, Alabama. He also served in the congress at Richmond, Virginia, but returned to Texas to organize the 7th Texas Infantry.

Although short in duration, the Battle of Raymond proved significant because it resulted in the disruption of field communications between Lt. Gen. John C. Pemberton, commander at Vicksburg, and his commanding officer, Gen. Joseph E. Johnston. Without clear orders on what actions to take next, the indecisive Pemberton in effect allowed Grant to dictate the overall direction of the campaign against Vicksburg, sealing the fate of the Confederate forces in the process.

The Monument

With the placement of a Texas in the Civil War monument near Raymond, the state once again became the first to offer commemoration of its forces at a key battlefield under development. The well-publicized dedication ceremony brought significant attention to local battlefield preservation efforts, thus resulting in much-needed funds to offset previous land purchase obligations. Key groups assisting the Texas Historical Commission with the planning for the monument were the Austin Civil War Round Table, headed by attorney Daniel M. Laney, and the Friends of Raymond, represented by president David H. McCain. Assisting with the marker inscription was Terry Winschel, the noted historian of Vicksburg National Military Park.

From the initial planning there were concerns about the location of the monument, particularly with regard to security and battlefield accessibility, as well as to the interpretive relevance to the role of the 7th Texas during the battle. The Friends of Raymond had acquired a small tract of land in the core area of fighting, but much of it was undeveloped

The Raymond monument "lies in state" in preparation for final placement by a crew from Stasswender Memorials of Austin. *Courtesy of Texas Historical Commission; Jim Stasswender, photographer.*

and not readily accessible to the traveling public. They had hoped to secure an easement on a larger tract of land where the Texans fought, but that conveyance failed to materialize. In the end, a private landowner along State Highway 18 agreed to provide a small easement for the placement of the Texas monument. There, state and local officials, reenactors and others, gathered on Saturday, May 4, 2000, for the dedication. Providing the keynote address that day was US Army Gen. Parker Hills (ret.), who spoke on the Battle of Raymond, with special attention to both the Texas and Mississippi forces who served with distinction on May 12, 1863.

The Texans

Central to the Confederate actions during the battle was the 7th Texas Infantry under command of Col. Hiram B. Granbury. On the back of the monument at Raymond, however, is a more extensive list of the Texas units who fought at various locales in the Vicksburg Campaign. They are, as noted on the monument:

Col. Hiram B. Granbury was a native of Copiah County, Mississippi, bordered on the north by Hinds County, where Raymond is located.

- 1st Texas Sharpshooters Battalion
- 2nd Texas Infantry Regiment
- 3rd Texas Cavalry Regiment
- 6th Texas Cavalry Regiment
- 6th Texas (Dismounted) Cavalry Regiment
- 7th Texas Infantry Regiment
- 9th Texas Cavalry Regiment
- 9th Texas Infantry Regiment

- 10th Texas (Dismounted) Cavalry Regiment
- 11th Texas Infantry Regiment
- 12th Texas Cavalry Regiment
- 12th Texas Infantry Regiment
- 13th Texas (Dismounted) Cavalry Regiment
- 14th Texas (Dismounted) Cavalry Regiment
- 14th Texas Infantry Regiment
- 16th Texas (Dismounted) Cavalry Regiment
- 16th Texas Infantry Regiment
- 17th Texas Infantry Regiment
- 18th Texas Infantry Regiment
- 19th Texas Infantry Regiment
- 21st Texas Cavalry Regiment
- 22nd Texas Infantry Regiment
- 27th Texas Cavalry Regiment
- 28th Texas (Dismounted) Cavalry Regiment
- 32nd Texas (Dismounted) Cavalry Regiment
- Bridges' Battalion
- Daniel's Battery
- Edgar's Battery
- Haldeman's Battery
- Pratt's Battery
- Waul's Texas Legion

Texans Remember

Colonel Granbury, for whom the Hood County seat of Granbury is named, died in the Battle of Franklin, Tennessee, on November 30, 1864. He was initially buried near Franklin but later reinterred near Columbia, Tennessee. Then, on November 30, 1893, his remains were again moved, this time to the Granbury Cemetery in Granbury, Texas, where his tombstone is inscribed with what his family believes is the correct spelling of his last name—Granberry.

Directions to Monument

Located south-southwest of Raymond on the east side of Highway 18 and just south of the Old Port Gibson Road, the monument sits in a landscaped area outside the right-of-way.

Suggested Readings

Winschel, Terrence. *Triumph and Defeat: The Vicksburg Campaign* (2 volumes). New York: Savas Beatie, 2004.

TEXAS

REMEMBERS THE VALOR
AND DEVOTION OF HER
SONS WHO SERVED AT
VICKSBURG AND IN OTHER
THEATERS OF THE WAR
BETWEEN THE STATES.
"FOR THOSE MEN BELIEVED
IN SOMETHING. THEY COUNTED
LIFE A LIGHT THING TO LAY
DOWN IN THE FAITH THEY BORE.
THEY WERE TERRIBLE IN
BATTLE. THEY WERE GENEROUS
IN VICTORY. THEY ROSE UP
FROM DEFEAT TO FIGHT
AGAIN, AND WHILE THEY
LIVED THEY WERE FORMIDABLE...
THE HERITAGE THEY LEFT,
OF VALOR AND DEVOTION
IS TREASURED BY A UNITED COUNTRY."
John W. Thomason, Jr.
THE SEALING OF THE BREACH

AT THIS LOCATION THE LINES
OF THE CONFEDERACY WERE
BROKEN AND THE TEXANS WERE
CALLED IN TO SEAL THE BREACH.
THEY NOT ONLY ACCOMPLISHED
THEIR MISSION BUT CAPTURED
A NUMBER OF THE ENEMY
AND SEIZED THEIR STANDARDS.

Siege of Vicksburg, Mississippi

December 1862–July 1863

The Situation

After winning a preliminary but significant victory at Raymond, Maj. Gen. Ulysses S. Grant found good reason to change his plans to take Vicksburg. Information reached him that Confederate reinforcements were arriving at the capital city of Jackson located no more than fifteen miles to his east. Further intelligence indicated that Gen. Joseph E. Johnston was also hurrying to Jackson to lead a coordinated attack on the Union force believed to be already heading west back toward Vicksburg. General Grant clearly had an effective spy network in place to give him such vital advance information about the plans of his enemy. Not only was he now alerted to General Johnston's impending arrival at Jackson, but he also learned that orders sent to Lt. Gen. John C. Pemberton at Vicksburg called for him to come out of his fortress to meet the Union advance head on. With this information, Grant decided to advance on Jackson, capture the city, and in so doing disrupt General Johnston's plans. The Confederate general, however, had a good spy system of his own. Upon hearing from one of his spies that Grant was heading toward Jackson instead of Vicksburg with a huge force that vastly outnumbered his own command, Johnston ordered the city abandoned. On May 14, the Union army occupied the city, suffering fewer than three hundred casualties. The next day, Grant ordered his men to turn their faces to the west toward Vicksburg, his long-desired objective on the Mississippi.

John C. Pemberton, a lieutenant general when he surrendered Vicksburg to Maj. Gen. Ulysses S. Grant on July 4, 1863, ended the war as a lieutenant colonel of artillery.

Roughly thirty-three thousand Union soldiers set out from Jackson. Even though Pemberton initially and perhaps wisely balked at Johnston's order to meet Grant's men at a point outside

Vicksburg, he finally obeyed his senior commander. There were twenty-two thousand men under Pemberton's command as it moved east to confront Grant.

On May 16, the two forces collided at Champion's Hill a short distance east of Vicksburg. The clash resulted in 2,500 Union casualties, with nearly 4,000 Confederate casualties reported. To some historians, the importance of the Battle of Champion's Hill has not been adequately recognized. It has even been claimed by some that the fight was the most decisive encounter of the entire Civil War. That bold assertion is apparently based on the fact that Vicksburg no longer had any chance of defying Grant's onslaught after Pemberton, having lost the Champion's Hill fight, could only retreat back into his fortress, there to await its inevitable capitulation. The ultimate loss of Vicksburg was without doubt one of the highly significant defeats that led directly to the downfall of the Confederacy nearly two years later. Perhaps it can be argued that the failure to stop Grant at Champion's Hill before he arrived at the fortress to lay siege was at least an important contributing factor in the eventual outcome of the siege itself. The actual battle at Champion's Hill, however, was not likely the most decisive battle of the entire Civil War.

On his way west to Vicksburg with Grant in pursuit, Pemberton did manage to mount a counterattack, but that also failed. By May 9, just four days after leaving Jackson, Grant's men surrounded Vicksburg on three sides, with the Mississippi River forming a natural barrier to escape on the west side of the fortress. The determined defenders nevertheless repeatedly thwarted Union attempts to overpower Vicksburg. On May 22, for example, Waul's Texas Legion, commanded by former Confederate congressman Thomas N. Waul, recaptured a position previously taken by federal forces in the early days of the assault. Discouraged by this and other vigorous efforts to deny direct entry into Vicksburg, Grant felt compelled to abandon his attack in favor of a time-consuming siege.

The siege began on May 25, 1863. There were still nearly thirty thousand Confederate troops within Vicksburg's walls, and by initiating highly effective artillery barrages they were determined to withstand the Union attack for as long as possible. In reality a continual firefight, the siege lasted for nearly fifty days. To ensure his quarry stayed essentially trapped inside the garrison, Grant called up reinforcements to bring his siege force to nearly eighty thousand troops. He used trenches, mines, and sharpshooters effectively in an effort to speed the collapse of the seemingly impregnable Confederate defensive stronghold.

The collapse finally came about on July 4, 1863, when General Pemberton surrendered his entire starving and sickness-ridden soldiers to General Grant. Shocked at the condition of his nearly thirty thousand prisoners, the Union general immediately paroled them all rather than send the Southerners to prison camps in the North. Although there was perhaps some degree of compassion behind Grant's actions, he also incorrectly assumed that few of the parolees, if any, would ever choose to fight against Union soldiers again. He further calculated that the time it would take to transfer such a horde of prisoners to camps back to the east could not be spared.

Grant's brilliant generalship, coupled with his relentless effort in conquering Vicksburg removed nearly all of the taint his reputation suffered following the Battle of Shiloh. US President Abraham Lincoln praised his fighting general, setting in motion the rapid rise of the now-famous battle-winning major general. Lincoln also fully recognized the vast importance of the fall of Vicksburg. The Mississippi was now a Union waterway dividing the Confederacy and presaging its demise. Grant himself perhaps best summed up his victory in his memoirs when he declared the capture of Vicksburg sealed the fate of the Confederacy. Many historians make much of the perhaps more famous Battle of Gettysburg as being the high water mark of the Southern Cause, but it was in fact the loss of Vicksburg that truly turned the tide of the war in favor of the Union.

> The disruption of Confederate military supply lines caused by the fall of Vicksburg increased the demand for Texas manufactured goods, including guns, gunpowder, and clothing.

The Texans

Among the many Texas units participating in the Vicksburg Campaign were:

- 2nd Texas Infantry Regiment
- Waul's Texas Legion
- 7th Texas Infantry Regiment
- 9th Texas Infantry Regiment
- 10th Texas Cavalry Regiment, Dismounted
- 14th Texas Cavalry Regiment, Dismounted
- 32nd Texas Cavalry Regiment, Dismounted
- 1st Texas Sharpshooters Battalion
- 3rd Texas Cavalry Regiment
- 6th Texas Cavalry Regiment
- 9th Texas Cavalry Regiment
- 27th Texas Cavalry Regiment
- Bridges' Battalion
- 16th Texas Infantry Regiment
- 17th Texas Infantry
- 19th Texas Infantry Regiment
- 16th Texas Cavalry Regiment, Dismounted
- 12th Texas Infantry Regiment
- 22nd Texas Infantry Regiment
- 18th Texas Infantry Regiment
- 14th Texas Infantry Regiment
- 11th Texas Infantry Regiment
- 6th Texas Cavalry Regiment, Dismounted
- 13th Texas Cavalry Regiment, Dismounted
- 12th Texas Cavalry Regiment
- Edgar's Battery

The Monument

By the 1890s, old regional tensions had changed, war veterans were getting older, and residential and commercial development already encroached on key battlefields, such as the one at Vicksburg. As might be expected, former states of the Confederacy were slow to join the commemorative efforts, and for many years only the home state of Mississippi had a monument at the site. Despite the reluctance, most participating states nevertheless reserved memorial sites within the park. For Texas there were two distinct choices— the Railroad Redoubt and the Texas Lunette—but only one truly viable, given postwar development of a cemetery near the latter. Although there were legislative efforts through the 1920s to commission a monument at Vicksburg, the necessary funding and private support failed to materialize, and it was not until the 1950s that the situation changed for two important reasons: the establishment of a historical agency, the Texas State Historical Survey Committee (TSHSC), to oversee such programs as monuments, and passage of a constitutional amendment authorizing the transfer of surplus money from the state's Confederate pension account to a state building fund. These two seemingly separate events nevertheless brought together both the mechanism and the money for Texas to place Civil War monuments.

Under the new system, Vicksburg became the front runner for a large monument of grand design, with other battlefields slated for more modest granite tablet monuments. On one level, the choice seems logical. With limited funds, the thinking went, the largest monument should be the one closest to Texas tourists that was located within a national park. Likewise, active veterans groups had pushed for the Vicksburg site. On the inside, though, there were other layers to the story. For years there was speculation that the impetus came from a governor, possibly Allan Shivers or Price Daniel, or maybe some advocacy from the United Daughters of the Confederacy. It seems, however, the choice came from what might at first appear as an unlikely source. The noted Civil War battlefield historian Ed Bearss was a young National Park Service (NPS) staffer at Vicksburg in the 1950s as Texas began planning the monument, and he believes the key player was state senator George "Cotton" Moffett of Hardeman County. At the time, Moffett was a powerful member of the Texas Legislature. A legislator since the 1930s, he was a sponsor of the bill that created the state historical committee, and he was also a history buff. As he noted in a 1961 letter to a constituent, "I had two grandfathers in the Confederate Army. Both of them saw action in battle several times and one was captured at Vicksburg and spent nearly two years in a prison camp."

Bearss recalls visiting with Senator Moffett at Vicksburg in 1956 and giving him a personal tour of a battlefield stop known as the Texas Circle. At the time, Moffett spoke of his grandfather's service at Vicksburg, as well as his friendship with Gen. Ashbel Smith of the 2nd Texas Infantry. Despite his ancestral connection to the battlefield, Moffett also believed it afforded the best opportunity for traveling Texans, located as it was along the celebrated Dixie Overland Highway.

This postrestoration picture shows how the grand design of architects Leonard Lundgren and Ed Maurer focused attention on Coe's lone Texan. The use of Texas granite for the backdrop and base adds to the uniqueness of the monument. *Courtesy of Texas Historical Commission.*

For the design of the Texas monument, the state commissioned the Austin architectural firm of Leonard Lundgren and Ed Maurer. TSHSC director George Hill suggested a semi-circular design of Texas Sunset Red granite. The architects' adaptation called for an approach of eleven steps, representing the sister states of the Confederacy, with a central monument of three sections and a central piece of statuary. Beaumont artist Herring Coe designed the lone soldier statue, depicting him carrying a rifle at the ready and resting a leg on the remains of a broken cannon. Standing on a five-sided granite star base, he is turned markedly to the left—not straight ahead—where he looks out across the battlefield several hundred yards toward the clearly visible 1906 Iowa monument. The juxtaposition of the two monuments across a site where soldiers of those two states met in battle in 1863 is, according to Bearss, unique among monumentation in national military parks and therefore presents a powerful interpretive statement.

Coe envisioned his lone Texan as a representation of the citizen soldier. In effect, the soldier came late to the battlefield, given the state's delay in funding, and so he is not pedestaled as with earlier statues but rather somewhat accessible, resting after a terrible ordeal and surveying the position he has retaken. Because accessibility was not always welcome when it came to statuary, though, the landscaping plan called for him to stand amid Spanish dagger yuccas to discourage those who would dare to join him at his post. (The plan also called for mass plantings of bluebonnets on the hillside, but the flowers

A large crowd gathered for the dedication of the Texas monument at the Railroad Redoubt in Vicksburg National Military Park, November 1961. Because the monument was not yet complete, only the center panel was in place at the time, supported by timbers. *Courtesy of Texas Historical Commission.*

failed to bloom in the acidic Mississippi soils.) The soldier does not evoke the swagger of Coe's Dick Dowling statue at Sabine Pass, Texas; instead, his shirt is open and his hat is scrunched up in front in a casual, nonmilitary manner. Quietly, he exhibits defiance, as if to say to the Iowans, "I've got my eyes on you. Don't try that again." In the end, Coe's lone Texan was not only late to the battlefield, but he was also late to his own monument, arriving at the site almost a year and half after the formal dedication in November 1961. Although the monument was still under construction at the time, with the massive center panel propped up by boards, the event went on as scheduled to take advantage of a national meeting of the United Daughters of the Confederacy in Jackson. Among those in attendance at the Railroad Redoubt that day were Texas Governor Price Daniel, Mississippi Governor Ross Barnett, and of course, Senator Moffett.

Shorty after the Texas Legislature created a Military Sites Program within the Texas Historical Commission (THC) in the 1990s, the staff began working in partnership with the NPS to restore the Vicksburg monument, which had fallen into disrepair through the years as a result of deterioration of the lettering, failed mortar joints, and the movement of steps. The legislature appropriated forty thousand dollars for the project and NPS personnel handled the construction following specifications drawn up by THC architect Stanley O. Graves. One significant change to the design was the gilding of the inscription, which NPS officials believed would last longer and be more legible. With completion of the work, THC and NPS representatives joined with a sizeable crowd of other celebrants and park visitors in rededicating the monument in 2001.

This photo shows the Texas monument undergoing recent restoration, a process funded by the Texas Legislature and under the direction of the Texas Historical Commission. The project included structural work, metalwork replacement, statuary cleaning and waxing, and the gilding of the inscription. *Courtesy of Texas Historical Commission.*

Texans Remember

Official Texas Historical Markers in three Texas counties—Galveston, Harris, and Comanche—commemorate the life of Dr. Ashbel Smith, one of the true giants of early Texas history and a veteran of Vicksburg. A native of Connecticut trained at Yale, he emigrated to the Republic of Texas and became friends with Sam Houston, who appointed him surgeon general of the army. Smith's career in Texas was extensive, with noteworthy service in medicine, government, education, and the military. Appointed a commissioner to establish what became Prairie View A&M University, he also served as president of the University of Texas, guiding early efforts of that institution to make it a world-class school with a medical school to match. Smith died in 1886 and is buried in the State Cemetery in Austin.

Directions to Monument

South loop of Confederate Avenue at the Railroad Redoubt, Vicksburg National Military Park, Vicksburg.

Suggested Readings

Ballard, Michael B. *Vicksburg: The Campaign that Opened the Mississippi.* Chapel Hill, NC: University of North Carolina Press, 2004.

Groom, Winston. *Vicksburg, 1863.* New York: Vintage Books, 2009.

Winschel, Terrence J. *Triumph and Defeat: The Vicksburg Campaign* (2 volumes). New York: Savas Beatie, 2004.

————. *Vicksburg: Fall of the Confederate Gibraltar.* Abilene, TX: McWhiney Foundation Press, 1999.

TEXAS

REMEMBERS THE VALOR AND DEVOTION OF
HER SONS WHO SERVED AT GETTYSBURG
JULY 2-3, 1863.

FROM NEAR THIS SPOT THE TEXAS BRIGADE
AT ABOUT 4:30 P.M. ON JULY 2, CROSSED
EMMITSBURG ROAD AND ADVANCED WITH
HOOD'S DIVISION ACROSS PLUM RUN TOWARD
LITTLE ROUND TOP. THE TEXAS BRIGADE
AFTER SEVERE FIGHTING ON THE SLOPES
OF LITTLE ROUND TOP RETIRED TO A
POSITION ON THE SOUTH SIDE OF DEVIL'S
DEN. THE BRIGADE HELD THIS POSITION THE
NIGHT OF JULY 2 AND DURING THE DAY OF
JULY 3. THE BRIGADE THEN FELL BACK TO A
POSITION NEAR THIS MEMORIAL ON THE
EVENING OF JULY 3. ON THE FIELD AT
GETTYSBURG THE TEXAS BRIGADE SUFFERED
597 CASUALTIES.
TEXAS TROOPS AT GETTYSBURG WERE
1ST TEXAS INF., LT. COL. P.A. WORK; 4TH
TEXAS INF., COL. J.C.G. KEY, LT. COL. B.F.
COL. R.M. POWELL, LT. COL. K. BRYAN, MAJ. J.C.
ROGERS. THE TEXAS BRIGADE INCLUDED THE
3RD ARKANSAS INF., COL. V. H. MANNING,
(BRIG. GEN. J.B. ROBERTSON'S TEXAS BRIGADE,
HOOD'S DIVISION, LONGSTREET'S CORPS).
OF ALL THE GALLANT FIGHTS THEY MADE,
NONE WAS GRANDER THAN GETTYSBURG

A MEMORIAL TO TEXANS
WHO SERVED THE CONFEDERACY

ERECTED BY THE STATE OF TEXAS 1963

Battle of Gettysburg, Pennsylvania

July 1–3, 1863

The Situation

In late spring 1863, the status of the Civil War was essentially a draw. As unlikely as that might have seemed to those many Northerners who had predicted the war would only last six months, the obvious fact was that the far more powerful North had failed to quickly crush the much weaker South. Aside from a few losses of its territory but an appalling loss of its young warriors, the Confederacy was still very much alive, and the North, hampered by less than brilliant generalship, seemed curiously impotent. Two major victories by Gen. Robert E. Lee's Army of Northern Virginia at Chancellorsville and Fredericksburg, Virginia, during the first week of May 1863 served to add potent fuel to Northern concerns. Although the losses in men and matériel suffered by the Confederacy in attaining those two key victories were more than the new nation could afford, the South did appear, at least on the surface, to have something of an upper hand as the summer drew near.

How to best capitalize on that illusory advantage was the prime concern of the Confederate leadership. Some felt that part of General Lee's victorious army should be dispatched to the west to break the siege then in progress at Vicksburg and perhaps drive the maddeningly persistent federal Maj. Gen. Ulysses S. Grant far away from that vital river fortress. At one point during the discussions, it was even suggested that Lee himself lead a campaign to rid Vicksburg of its Union foe. General Lee, however, had a plan of his own. Though keenly aware of the importance of Vicksburg and its ability to control traffic on the vital Mississippi River, Lee firmly believed a direct full-scale invasion of the North would not only help alleviate pressure on the fortress but also accomplish much more for the Confederate cause in the east at the same time. His first invasion of Northern territory in September 1862 ended with a Union victory at Sharpsburg rather than a glorious march of his army into Washington, DC, as he had envisioned. The ever-optimistic and always-aggressive Lee, however, convinced himself, along with President Jefferson Davis and other key Southern leaders, that a second invasion was both militarily promising and potentially politically rewarding.

Lee's rationale was much as it had been before he had crossed the Potomac into Maryland some eight months previously. Once again he envisioned the benefits of taking the ruinous fighting away from his beloved Virginia and onto the supply-rich turf of his enemy. Once there, he believed he would easily be able to win a decisive victory and cause the ever-growing antiwar sentiments in the North to overflow into a peace offer that would allow the South to be forever free of the United States of America. In the process, European powers might well then formally recognize the new Confederate nation so all the dreams of that nation would at last come to pass. Of more immediate value would be the wholesale disruption of Union military activities elsewhere in view of the strong possibility that Lee's apparently indomitable Army of Northern Virginia might any day crash through strong defensive lines to conquer the US capital city of Washington. Too, there was always that keen hope that many of the Union forces called upon to hurry east to protect their capital would be drawn from the siege lines surrounding Vicksburg now pinioning it to the river it still so effectively guarded and controlled.

With its two recent significant victories, the Army of Northern Virginia and particularly its brilliant commander had an unshakeable confidence in its ability to bring the already costly war to a satisfactory conclusion. The May victories had helped increase the combat-depleted size of the army back to nearly its original strength of seventy-five thousand through new enlistments, but one casualty in the woods near Chancellorsville still cast a dark shadow across the high spirits of Lee and his men. The loss of Lt. Gen. Thomas J. (Stonewall) Jackson to friendly fire during that victorious battle deprived Lee of his most able senior lieutenant. In the weeks soon to come, the absence of the eccentric but highly resourceful Jackson would be sorely felt in the Army of Northern Virginia and throughout the entire South.

In his first battle as General Jackson's replacement, Lt. Gen. Richard Ewell showed considerable tactical promise. His success during the second battle, at Winchester, Virginia, on June 15, 1863, cleared the way for General Lee's army to begin its invasion of Pennsylvania, well within the borders of the now-invaded US territory. By the end of June, all the Army of Northern Virginia had arrived in the state. At this point, the future for the invasion seemed promising. The initial military objective of Lee's invasion was the key rail center of Harrisburg, Pennsylvania. Tracks emanated south out of Harrisburg toward both Baltimore and Washington. Any plans to move against those two key cities would require the logistical support that only railroads could efficiently and effectively provide.

The first in a long series of events that would affect Lee's plans occurred soon after his army had crossed into the North. The flamboyant cavalier, Maj. Gen. J. E. B. Stuart, had only recently suffered an embarrassment when his brigades had been surprised by an unexpected attack by Union cavalry. In an effort to regain the confidence of General Lee and to reestablish his well-earned, if now somewhat tarnished, reputation as a bold cavalier, Stuart embarked on what was intended to be an absolutely vital reconnaissance of all Union forces in the region. To prove to Lee that he was capable of doing far more than just merely reporting on enemy troop concentrations, if any did indeed exist, Stuart began an encircling ride that took his troopers far into enemy territory. Then, he believed, he would be in the enviable position of telling Lee of his daring exploits and thus be returned to his favor. It was, however, not to be. With Stuart off on his dramatic jaunt, Lee was left completely blind as far as the disposition of any potential enemy force was concerned. As it developed, there was in fact an enemy force nearby, fully aware of Lee's presence on Union turf. Not until June 28, 1863, did the Virginian learn that a federal army some ninety-five thousand-men strong had trailed him across Pennsylvania, awaiting a rare opportunity to entrap and do battle with an invading force hindered by only tenuous logistical support.

The Union's Army of the Potomac, biding its time before attacking Lee far from its supply points, had initially been led by Maj. Gen. Joseph Hooker, who recently had been outgeneraled by Lee at Chancellorsville. Displeased by both Hooker's apparent incompetence and even more obvious bombast, US President Abraham Lincoln removed him and replaced him with Maj. Gen. George Gordon Meade, with whom Lee had served only fifteen years previously during the Mexican War. Meade soon learned that Lee's army had split into several parts as it marched across Pennsylvania. To force Lee to fight without his usual careful advance appraisal of the terrain and the conditions that would shape the battle, Meade planned to strike one element of the invading army and then pounce upon the balance of it when Lee rushed all of his forces to relieve the embattled element under attack.

Upon learning of the Union army's presence, the wily Lee hastened to consolidate his entire army before Meade could accomplish what he intended. The place of consolidation chosen by Lee was in the vicinity of Cashtown and the small university town of Gettysburg, Pennsylvania. Even as his army rapidly regrouped, Lee apparently considered abandoning his invasion and going back, with his army still intact, to Virginia to fight another day. Uncharacteristically surprised and still blinded as a result of Stuart's escapade, the commanding general faced several problems. First, the fight that loomed was not likely to be fought as he always preferred. It was Lee who would have to make the initial move, rather than wait for his opponent to make a mistake. Second, he could not afford to wait because of the danger to his supply lines so vital to any invasion scheme. Finally, he could not retreat as he had so briefly considered because to do so was to admit that the whole second invasion idea had been a poor one. Having convinced himself that the battle at hand was better than going back to Virginia, and buoyed by his confidence in the invincibility of the Army of Northern Virginia, General Lee moved toward Gettysburg and General Meade's Army of the Potomac.

The Battle

On July 1, 1863, two Confederate divisions moved toward Gettysburg to reconnoiter the placement of Meade's forces. The soldiers also were intent on foraging for a much-needed supply of shoes said to be in the region. They soon encountered Union army pickets and the first clash of the Battle of Gettysburg ensued just west of that small town. Reinforcements for both sides quickly responded to the sound of gunfire, and the engagement soon became more heated. In time, the intense fighting forced the Union men to retreat through the city and take up defensive positions on Cemetery Hill south of town. There, the Confederate forward movement stalled. Fatigued, both sides ceased firing as the sun set. By next morning, both the Army of Northern Virginia and the Union's Army of the Potomac had arrived on the scene in full force. Both sides suffered heavy losses as the Union established its line from Culp's Hill to the Round Tops through a series of attacks and counterattacks at such now well-known sites as the Devil's Den and Little Round Top.

At the end of the second day of fighting, General Meade considered withdrawing from the field at Gettysburg. Although his men had satisfactorily repulsed several strong attacks on both the left and right of his line of defense, there was no guarantee he could withstand another full-scale attack, particularly given the severity of his losses. However, his staff soon convinced him that it would be far wiser to stand and fight an equally depleted foe than to retreat, only to have Lee, no matter how weakened, in close pursuit even deeper into Northern territory. Meade himself, with the quick concurrence of his staff, determined that Lee, having just failed to breach both the left and right of the Union line, would next hurl his full force against the center of that line, now firmly entrenched on Cemetery Ridge.

The next day proved Meade to be absolutely correct. Lee ordered Lt. Gen. James Longstreet to prepare to charge across a wide field of to overrun the Union center. Often querulous, Longstreet disagreed with Lee and disagreed vehemently. The ensuing debate between the commanding general and his habitually sulking lieutenant cost valuable time as the hot July sun rose higher and higher over the wheat field. The Confederate charge finally came, despite Longstreet's nearly insubordinate refusal to move with any degree of haste. Hours after its intended time, what became known as Pickett's Charge commenced under a bright sun and in oppressive heat. Some 12,500 men began moving toward the Union position across the field. A massive Confederate artillery barrage, which some said could be heard nearly 150 miles away in Pittsburgh, ceased just before the charge. Although a reported nine of every ten Confederate shells landed well behind the Union position, the Southern gunners believed their barrage had been effective enough to put the answering enemy barrage out of action. Actually, the North's artillerymen had simply halted their firing in anticipation of the infantry charge that would likely soon be coming their way.

Their wait was not long. As the Confederates began to run, shrieking the now famous rebel yell, federal guns opened fire. As General Lee and his reluctant lieutenant Longstreet looked on from Seminary Ridge, his soldiers fell as though being scythed. Onward they rushed, their numbers dwindling by the second, even though at least some of them reached the Union ramparts. There, outnumbered and fatigued from heat and shattered by deafening and deadly shells and then small arms fire, their charge that has come to define the entire Battle of Gettysburg, if not the Lost Cause of the Confederacy itself, dwindled to become at first a halt and then a full retreat. Of the 12,500 who charged against the Union lines under the proud eyes of Lee, only 5,000 made it back to where he now sat on his horse in grieved silence. Out of thirty regimental battle flags, nineteen were in the hands of the victorious Union troops.

Brig. Gen. John Bell Hood led Texas forces in fierce fighting at Devil's Den and Little Round Top during the Battle of Gettysburg. He was severely wounded in the left arm during the action and removed from the battlefield. He never regained full use of the arm. *Courtesy of Library of Congress, LC-B813-6594-B.*

With Lee stunned, Longstreet devastated, and the whole invasion in total disarray and grim defeat, the only thing left to do was prepare for Meade to launch an attack of his own and destroy, once and for all, the heretofore allegedly invincible Army of Northern Virginia. Meade, however, did not come. Although his inaction earned him the lasting enmity of President Lincoln, most historians believe the general was wise not to pursue Lee back across the Potomac. At any rate, Lee did leave Pennsylvania in an orderly retreat on July 14, 1863. He would never again be able to mount a full-scale offensive operation during the war. He lost seventeen of his generals in the battle, with six of them killed, eight wounded, and three captured during the fighting. Even worse, his army of 75,000 suffered 28,063 casualties, more than a third of his original force. To be sure, the Union had been hit almost equally as hard. Out of the 88,000 engaged, 23,049 fell; but the North's potential for replacements was still strong, whereas the Confederacy would soon find precious few willing to reenlist following this defeat.

The actual significance of the Battle of Gettysburg did not emerge until much later. Perhaps President Lincoln sensed its importance before most others, using the battlefield as the setting for the most stirring speech of his presidency. The war was to rage on for two more dreadful years. After Gettysburg and the almost simultaneous fall of Vicksburg in the west, however, the eventual outcome, costly though it would prove to be, was never in doubt.

Brig. Gen. Felix Huston Robertson, son of Brig. Gen. Jerome B. Robertson, was the only native Texan to achieve the rank of general in the Confederate army. He was also the last surviving Confederate general officer upon his death in April 1928. Like his father, he is buried in Waco, Texas.

As in any so important and decisive defeat, Southern leaders soon launched an orchestrated effort to determine who was to blame. Characteristically, Lee volunteered to take the brunt of that blame upon himself. Desolate at his loss, he offered to resign, but President Davis would not hear of it. Unlike the often benevolent and forgiving Davis, historians have analyzed the battle for more than a century and a half, seeking someone to hold culpable for the South's debacle at Gettysburg. Even Lee's most ardent biographer, who usually hints that the iconic general could have walked across the Potomac River even at flood stage, admits it was his second poorest performance. Others contend that if only Jackson had been present at the battle, things would have certainly gone much better for the Confederacy. Others insist that if Longstreet had only been willing to follow his commander's orders without question, or if Stuart had not gone on his vainglorious ride around Pennsylvania, the results at the battlefield would have been far different.

It seems likely, though, that General Lee himself had been right when he claimed the defeat was all of his own making. His key orders during the battle were not precise, and he gave his subordinates too much latitude when latitude could not be afforded. Most of all, he zealously and foolishly believed his beloved Army of Northern Virginia might truly be invincible. To be sure, Lee did not get what he needed from his senior commanders at Gettysburg, but in the final analysis he was in overall command, and the loss is forever his to bear.

The Texans

Among the Texas Units participating in the Battle of Gettysburg were:
- 1st Texas Infantry Regiment, Lt. Col. P. A. Work commanding
- 4th Texas Infantry Regiment, Col. J. C. Key, Lt. Col. B. F. Carter, and Maj. J. P. Bane commanding
- 5th Texas Infantry Regiment, Col. R. M. Powell, Lt. Col. K. Bryan, and Maj. J. C. Rogers commanding

All were part of Brig. Gen. Jerome B. Robertson's Texas Brigade, Hood's Division, Longstreet's Corps.

Author Thomas E. Alexander at the Texas monument during a 2012 tour of Gettysburg National Military Park. *Courtesy of Alexander Collection.*

The Monument

Located on South Confederate Avenue in Gettysburg National Military Park, the Texas monument interprets the site from which the Texas Brigade began its advance to Little Round Top on July 2, 1863. It was a site the Texans would grow to know well because it held the position through the evening of July 3, despite intense fighting and a high casualty count. The monument dates from a century after the battle, and over time, the darkened letters faded, with the text virtually impossible to read. In 1997, the survey team of the Texas Historical Commission met with staff of the Friends of the National Parks at Gettysburg and asked for assistance in restoring the monument. In a true reflection of national unity and cooperation, the Texas delegation worked with the Pennsylvania-based organization and volunteers from Burlington, New Jersey, to refurbish the Confederate monument in 1998.

Texans Remember

Winkler County in far West Texas is named for Clinton McKamey Winkler, wounded in action at Gettysburg. Born in North Carolina, he moved to the Republic of Texas in 1840, and following statehood became a legislator. During the Civil War, he raised a company that joined the 4th Texas Infantry of Hood's Brigade. He became a commander as a lieutenant colonel and participated with the unit in various battles until the end of the war, when he was among the Confederate forces surrendering with General Lee at Appomattox Court House in Virginia. Afterward, he returned to Texas and served in the legislature and was one of the first jurists on the state court of appeals. Two state historical markers commemorate the contributions of Winkler. One is on the courthouse square in Kermit, seat of government for the county named in his honor. The other is at his gravesite in Oaklawn Cemetery in Corsicana, Navarro County.

Directions to Monument

South Confederate Avenue off Emmitsburg Road (US 15), Gettysburg National Military Park.

Suggested Readings

Sears, Stephen W. *Gettysburg*. New York: Houghton Mifflin, 2004.

Skoch, George, and Mark W. Perkins. *Lone Star Confederate: A Gallant and Good Soldier of the 5th Texas Infantry*. College Station: Texas A&M University Press, 2003.

TEXAS

REMEMBERS THE VALOR AND DEVOTION OF
HER SONS WHO SERVED AT CHICKAMAUGA
SEPTEMBER 19-20, 1863.

HERE IN THE GREAT CONFEDERATE BREAK-
THROUGH TEXANS VIED WITH EACH OTHER
TO PROVE THEMSELVES WORTHY OF THE FAME
WON BY THEIR BROTHERS ON OTHER FIELDS.

. . . .

ERECTED BY THE STATE OF TEXAS 1964

Battle of Chickamauga, Georgia

September 18–20, 1863

The Situation

Although he was not a West Point–trained military strategist, US President Abraham Lincoln had a plan he believed would ultimately win the Civil War. In his view, the key to victory lay only in the decisive annihilation of all Confederate armies rather than in the often temporary capture of enemy real estate. On July 4, 1863, it appeared his plan was at last succeeding. Gen. Robert E. Lee's Army of Northern Virginia suffered its first significant defeat at Gettysburg. Even though Maj. Gen. George Gordon Meade failed to pursue and perhaps destroy Lee's crippled army, he put it on a defensive course from which it would never fully recover. Angry as he was with Meade's reluctance to deliver a potential death blow to Lee's still legendary army, Lincoln was satisfied the Army of the Potomac was now draining away the lifeblood of the enemy in the war's Eastern Theater.

On the very same day Meade prevailed at Gettysburg, Lincoln's rising star in the West had, at long last, captured the vital Confederate river fortress at Vicksburg, Mississippi. To be sure, it took Maj. Gen. Ulysses S. Grant an inordinate amount of time to finally overpower the South's most formidable citadel, but he managed to do so without sustaining massive losses of manpower. Although far more Confederate troops were captured (and then released, much to Lincoln's chagrin) than had been killed, the military situation in the West was now clearly under Union control. With both the Eastern and the Western theaters succumbing to federal pressure and with Confederate losses mounting to near irreversible levels, it now remained only for the Union to cripple permanently the Confederate presence in Tennessee and Kentucky to set the final stage for the winning of the war.

Integral to this campaign was the capture of the key city of Chattanooga, Tennessee. It was not necessarily the city itself that made it so important to Union strategists but rather its importance as a vital railroad junction. From its rail terminus ran the tracks of the Nashville & Chattanooga, the East Tennessee and Georgia line leading to Virginia, and the Western & Atlantic Railway Company with its key access to Atlanta, Georgia. To capture those rail lines was to block the main arteries of supply that helped sustain the Confederacy and at the same time gain the means of transporting Union soldiers into the heartland of the South.

Union Brig. Gen. James A. Garfield was chief aide to General William S. Rosecrans during the Battle of Chickamauga. He survived the war only to be assassinated in September 1881 while serving as president of the United States.

The challenge to accomplishing this important objective fell to Maj. Gen. William S. Rosecrans. The general earned President Lincoln's admiration in July 1863 when he skillfully maneuvered the Confederate forces of Gen. Braxton Bragg out of their formations at Tullahoma, Tennessee, sustaining only minimal casualties. Flushed from Middle Tennessee by Rosecrans's brilliant tactics, Bragg pulled his Army of Tennessee back to Chattanooga to defend the railway center from the Union advance sure to come. Rosecrans did not disappoint the irascible Bragg. Dividing his army into three columns to make its way through the narrow passes of the Cumberland Mountains, the Union general finally arrived at Chattanooga but only after a delay of nearly six weeks. Beginning to exhibit an unfortunate McClellan-like tendency to be overly cautious, Rosecrans explained to Washington that it had taken more than forty days to travel the roughly seventy miles to Chattanooga to wait for the supplies he felt he would require to defeat Bragg and capture the city.

As the situation developed, the delay proved to be unwarranted and, at least initially, the supplies unnecessary. Although Bragg's forces outnumbered the approaching Union army, the Confederate general once again fell victim to one of Rosecrans's clever troop movement ruses and feints. By September 8, 1863, all of Bragg's men left Chattanooga without firing a shot and slipped away into Georgia less than ten miles to the south.

At this point, all of Rosecrans's tactical similarities with the hapless Maj. Gen. George B. McClellan seemed to dissolve in the heady exhilaration generated by having taken his important objective without any significant shedding of Northern blood. Holding back a sizeable force of twenty thousand men in reserve to bolster the conquered city's defenses against any future enemy attack, Rosecrans sent eighty thousand of his men in hot pursuit of Bragg's army believing the Confederates to be in full retreat upon leaving Chattanooga. Rosecrans did not know, however, that Bragg waited for him less than twenty miles south of Chattanooga with some fifty thousand men, eager to spring a trap, which Union intelligence had failed to detect. To make matters worse for the suddenly rash Rosecrans, his three corps were essentially out of touch with each other and rushing into the trap spread out over fifty miles.

All Bragg had to do was wait for the entire Army of the Cumberland to be ensnared and then destroyed. The troubled Confederate general, however, found a way to unset his own trap. Such varied issues as a near-mutinous staff of senior officers who fought among themselves every bit as vigorously as they each did with their commanding general, an almost total lack of respect from his own men, a siege of boils and chronic diarrhea, plus an oft-repeated habit of blaming others for his own mistakes, contributed to Bragg's failure to capitalize on General Rosecrans's uncharacteristic exuberance. Repeated efforts by Confederate cavalry brigades to surprise and annihilate the advancing Union force before it could regroup and be concentrated in one strong position failed, largely as a result of the constant squabbling among Bragg's lieutenants, as well as poor staff work.

Alerted to the surprise trap that could not now be sprung, Rosecrans drew his

At great cost of resources, Gen. Braxton Bragg led the Confederate Army of Tennessee against the Army of the Cumberland under Maj. Gen. William S. Rosecrans at both Stones River and Chickamauga. Following the war, Bragg moved to Galveston, Texas, to oversee railroad construction. He died there of a brain seizure in 1876. *Courtesy of the Library of Congress, LC- B813- 6579 [P&P].*

command into battle position in the dense woods along Georgia's West Chickamauga Creek, less than twenty miles south of Chattanooga. Bragg's men had already formally established their opposing lines, setting the stage for the brutal Battle of Chickamauga.

The Battle

Accounts differ as to just how many effectives were enjoined in the battle, but the most likely source puts the Union force at sixty-two thousand, with the Confederates fielding sixty-six thousand. Some reports indicate Rosecrans might actually have had some five thousand fewer troops in the battle. Bragg's relative superiority in numbers had come about by a sizeable reinforcement coming from the ranks of the still-reeling Army of Northern Virginia, commanded by no less than Lt. Gen. James Longstreet, likely pleased and relieved to get away from now widely heard public speculation that his hesitancy had poorly served General Lee at Gettysburg two months previous. The arrival of Longstreet's ten thousand-plus force clearly negated some of the validity of President Lincoln's attack-the-enemy-army strategy that had otherwise worked so well. Lincoln believed that a Confederate army fully occupied by opposing federal forces would be unable to send reinforcements to another Confederate force being similarly faced by its enemy. Recognizing the importance of securing Chattanooga from Union control, Confederate President Jefferson Davis had initially asked the temporarily dispirited General Lee to replace Bragg in command soon after Gettysburg fell. When Lee refused, Davis sent his next best man, Longstreet, to save Bragg from both General Rosecrans and himself.

Without Longstreet's intervention and the help of the Confederate bishop-general Leonidas Polk, Bragg likely would have completely failed to make the most of Rosecrans's hurriedly established lines of battle south of Chattanooga. The night before the battle had been filled with a constant shifting of troops in the dark woods, and neither side knew for certain just where their enemy's position was weak enough to permit penetration. As the battle line stretched nearly six miles in length, Bragg understandably found it difficult at daybreak to determine if his original assumption about the weakness of the Union's defensive position remained valid. Nevertheless, after hours of futile and bloody attacks and counterattacks against strong lines of defense, the first full day of fighting proved to have gained nothing for either side.

Confederate Lt. Gen. Leonidas Polk, an Episcopal bishop before the war, was court-martialed following the Battle of Chickamauga because General Braxton Bragg accused him of disobeying orders. Cleared of all charges, General Polk died in action at Pine Mountain, Georgia, on June 14, 1864.

The next day turned out to be a lucky one for General Longstreet but an unlucky one for General Polk, a close friend of Davis, classmate of the fallen Albert Sidney Johnston, and a West Point graduate turned Episcopal bishop. Although ordered by Bragg to attack the Union line early in the morning of September 20, with Longstreet on the left and Polk on the right, the appointed hour of the Confederate charge came and went because of the absence of General Polk. When he finally arrived on the scene, the assault on enemy lines at last commenced in full fury. Rested by the Confederate delay, and by then also well aware of the enemy's intentions, the Union troops handily repulsed the charge, but with heavy losses taken on both sides of the often hand-to-hand conflict.

Furious at the delay and the resulting failure of the attack, Bragg ordered Longstreet to hit the Union center at full force. The luck that had eluded Longstreet at Gettysburg finally came to his aid in the Chickamauga woods. The tardy General Polk made good progress in rolling the Union left, and observing this, Rosecrans hurriedly sent a brigade from his right to stop Polk's advance. For a few minutes, this shift in manpower created a gap in the Union lines, and Longstreet quickly noted the inviting pathway thus created into the heart of the entire Union position. Hesitant no more, he sent five divisions pouring through the gap, causing the federal line to buckle and collapse in panic. Everything Rosecrans had, including his dignity and his military reputation, was swept away in the flood of yelling rebels. The general, his staff, a third of his army, four division commanders, and three corps commanders fled before the Confederate tidal wave, not stopping until they had raced all the way back to Chattanooga. Longstreet then asked Bragg for more men to continue the rout. Had Bragg consented to this reasonable enough request, Chattanooga, yielded to Rosecrans without issue just days previously, likely could have been retaken from the disorganized and rattled Union force. As it was, however, the Battle of Chickamauga led instead to an ultimately meaningless Confederate siege of Chattanooga. History would show that although Bragg won a tactical victory, nothing of lasting importance came of it. Had he given Longstreet the men he needed to make the battle a rewarding one, the long-range effect would have been different. Instead, Bragg gained the lasting and often vitriolic enmity of Longstreet, as well as that of Polk and especially that of the fiery Nathan Bedford Forrest, who had chafed at the bit to pursue Rosecrans and reclaim Chattanooga.

Brig. Gen. John Bell Hood, the famed commander of Hood's Texas Brigade, was wounded at Chickamauga and lost his left leg as a result. General Hood's arm had been severely injured during the fighting at Gettysburg two months previously.

The casualties were immense on both sides, making it the bloodiest battle in the entire Western Theater. The Union reported losses of 16,170 and the Confederacy 18,454, each number representing almost exactly 28 percent of the effectives involved on both sides. It was the largest as well as the final victory, as such, for the Confederacy, but it did precious little to do anything for the Southern cause except delay its final collapse. To be sure, the military careers of all those Union generals who deserted the field in front of Longstreet's surging divisions remained tainted beyond repair. General Grant, just promoted to command all Union forces between the Appalachian Mountains and the Mississippi River, arrived on the scene to relieve the still-stunned General Rosecrans from command. He was replaced by Maj. Gen. George H. Thomas, the "Rock of Chickamauga," who alone among all Union commanders on the field on the second day rallied his troops to stand and fight. As for the Confederates, perhaps Maj. Gen. D. H. Hill said it best, "The barren victory at Chickamauga sealed the fate of the Confederacy."

The Texans

Among the Texas units fighting at Chickamauga were:
- 7th Texas Infantry Regiment
- 10th Texas Infantry Regiment
- 17th Texas Cavalry, Dismounted
- 18th Texas Cavalry, Dismounted
- 24th Texas Cavalry, Dismounted
- 25th Texas Cavalry Dismounted
- Douglas's Texas Artillery

All were part of Deshler's Brigade, Cleburne's Division.

- 9th Texas Infantry Regiment
- 10th Texas Cavalry, Dismounted
- 14th Texas Cavalry, Dismounted

All were part of Ector's Brigade, Walker's Division.

- 7th Texas Infantry Regiment

Gregg's Brigade, Johnson's Division

- 1st Texas Infantry Regiment
- 4th Texas Infantry Regiment
- 5th Texas Infantry Regiment

All were part of Robertson's Brigade, Hood's Division.

- 8th Texas Cavalry
- 11th Texas Cavalry

Both part of Harrison's Brigade, Wharton's Division.

The Monument

The Chickamauga battlefield landscape, like others in the National Park Service (NPS), is dotted with numerous plaques and markers depicting troop movements and positions throughout the duration of the battle. Many are detailed in scope, providing landmark time and positioning information, such as one for Ector's Brigade which notes:

> The brigade arrived at Jay's Mill from the vicinity of Alexander's house soon after 9 a.m. It formed on the left of Dibrell's Brigade and attacked the front of Van Derbeer's Brigade of Brannan's Division. The fighting continued with severity till about 11 o'clock when the brigade was obliged to retire, its left flank in the withdrawal coming under fire of the left battalions of King's Brigade or Baird's Division then just relieving Croxton's Brigade of Brannan's Division. It halted in the vicinity of Jay's Mill until near sundown and was not further engaged. (Marker is located 200 feet south of Reed's Bridge Road near the Second Minnesota Monument.)

The purpose of these so-called field markers, many of which the War Department placed when it oversaw park operations through the early part of the twentieth century, was twofold: to allow visitors to view sites—the "hallowed ground"—where their ancestors actually served and died and to allow military historians to plot troop movements in their studies of war tactics and strategies. Chickamauga was one of the most successful field study areas under the War Department, and when the agency transferred the site to the NPS in the early 1930s, there were about one thousand markers, plaques, and monuments

This c. 1918 photograph of heritage tourists at Chickamauga and Chattanooga National Military Park serves as a reminder of the historic role such battlefield sites have played in US society for generations. *Library of Congress, LC-F8-1533.*

already in place. Many others, including the Texas monument, have been added since that time.

The interpretive text on the state's monument at Chickamauga is particularly brief—and surprisingly vague—including only one sentence beyond the introductory line: "Here in the great Confederate breakthrough Texans vied with each other to prove themselves worthy of the fame won by the their brothers on other fields." The rest of the text field on both the front and back of the monument is given over to the list of Texas units; there is no interpretive site-specific information. Perhaps, given the number of field markers already in place by the 1960s, state officials saw no need to elaborate on the information already in place. Regardless, the monument is decidedly commemorative and less educational in scope than other Texas battlefield monuments, especially those placed since 1998.

The staffs of the Chickamauga and Chattanooga National Military Park and the Texas Historical Commission (THC) worked closely to establish the guidelines for the monument's restoration in 1998, and NPS personnel conducted the work. As the park's Chief of Facilities, Charles E. Thomas, noted in a December 2, 1999, letter to the THC, "We have completed all phases of the project to rehab the Texas monument. . . . The project has greatly improved the appearance of the monument. All work was completed by the park painter (William Dorsey). . . ."

Texans Remember

The University of Texas is today a world-class institution of higher learning, in part as a result of the vision and early philanthropic support of Maj. George Washington Littlefield (1842–1920), a veteran of Chickamauga. The Mississippi native came to Texas with his parents in 1850 and grew up on a plantation in Gonzales County. Wounded in the war, he returned to Texas in 1864 and by the early 1870s was among those cattlemen driving herds to the railhead in Abilene, Kansas. Through his ranching interests and his understanding of the value of water rights, he helped open large sections of West Texas and New Mexico to cattle production, making famous his LIT and LFD brands in the process. He also founded the town of Littlefield, the county seat of Lamb County, northwest of Lubbock in West Texas.

Littlefield expanded his business base through the years and became a prominent banker in Austin. He used his considerable wealth to support a wide range of educational interests, including the study of Southern history, hoping to avoid what he believed was "Northern bias," particularly about the Civil War. Appointed to the University of Texas Board of Regents in 1911, he gave generously of his money, property, vast historical collections, and extensive personal library in support of the school. Today, landmarks on the campus include the ornate Littlefield Fountain, the Littlefield Dorm (funded in honor of his wife, Alice), and the Littlefield House.

Directions to Monument

Battleline Road south of Alexander Bridge Road, Chickamauga and Chattanooga National Military Park. Inquire at visitor center, 3370 Lafayette Road, Fort Oglethorpe, Georgia.

Suggested Readings

Cozzens, Peter. *This Terrible Sound: The Battle of Chickamauga.* Urbana: University of Illinois Press, 1992.

Woodworth, Steven. *Six Armies in Tennessee: The Chickamauga and Chattanooga Campaigns.* Lincoln: University of Nebraska Press, 1998.

————, ed. *The Chickamauga Campaign.* Carbondale: University of Southern Illinois Press, 2010.

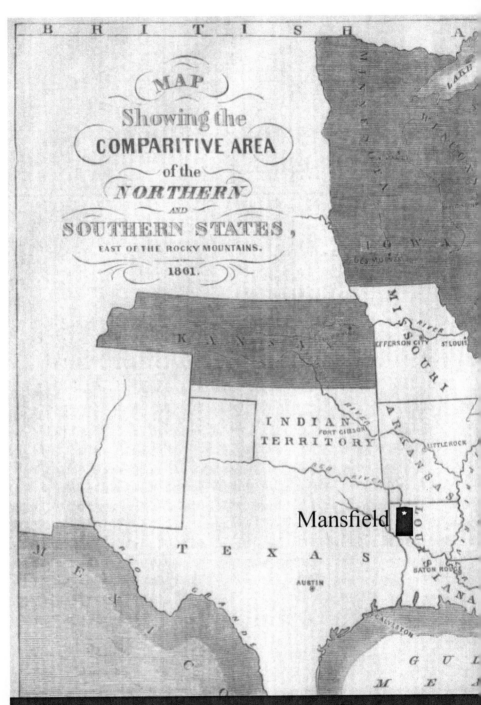

MAP
Showing the
COMPARITIVE AREA
of the
NORTHERN
AND
SOUTHERN STATES,
EAST OF THE ROCKY MOUNTAINS.
1861.

Mansfield

Ulysses S. Grant don't scare worth a damn.
—*Soldier of the 5th Wisconsin Infantry*

1864

The Wilderness

Kennesaw Mountain

Hurrah for Texas!
—*Robert E. Lee*

TEXAS

REMEMBERS HER SONS BY WHOSE VALOR AND
DEVOTION THE FEDERAL ENEMY WAS DEFEATED
AT MANSFIELD, APRIL 8, 1864 AND
THEREAFTER IN SEVERAL BLOODY
ENGAGEMENTS DRIVEN FROM THE RED RIVER
VALLEY. THUS WAS TEXAS SAVED FROM THE
PHYSICAL RUIN WROUGHT BY THE WAR IN
EVERY OTHER SOUTHERN STATE.

. . . .

A MEMORIAL TO TEXANS WHO SERVED THE CONFEDERACY

ERECTED BY THE STATE OF TEXAS 1963

Battle of Mansfield, Louisiana

Also known as Battle of Sabine Cross Roads

April 8, 1864

The Situation

The enthronement of Maximilian as the French emperor of Mexico on June 12, 1862, added to US President Abraham Lincoln's already heavy burden. The distinct possibility of French military adventurers flowing across the Rio Grande into Confederate Texas made it important to raise the flag of the United States somewhere in that breakaway state. To do so would hopefully discourage any schemes France might have to take advantage of the strife and confusion created by the Civil War that was currently being waged between the states. The fact was that France had clearly ignored the Monroe Doctrine in coming to Mexico in the first place. Further, the knowledge that the Confederacy had long been doing a brisk business with Mexico trading cotton for guns compelled Lincoln to take immediate measures to reclaim at least some token part of the Lone Star State.

Acting upon Lincoln's orders, Maj. Gen. Nathaniel P. Banks began a campaign up the Red River section in Louisiana to overpower Confederate positions on the Texas section of the river. Once there, he planned to raise the US flag as a message to France that even though Texas was for the moment out of the Union, it was still part of the North American entity protected by the Monroe Doctrine.

The attempt to take the Texas river installation at Sabine Pass on September 8, 1863, proved to be futile despite the use and overwhelming firepower of US Navy gunboats. The dogged determination and accurate gunnery of the Texan defenders quickly foiled Union plans to land thousands of troops on Texas soil after the gunboats' artillery had nullified

Nathaniel P. Banks served as Massachusetts governor, Congressman, and US Speaker of the House before the Civil War and hoped to use his military experience for even greater political gain following the conflict. Although his defeats at Sabine Pass and Mansfield failed to help in that regard, voters in his home state of Massachusetts returned him to Congress after the war. *Courtesy of Library of Congress, LC-USZ62-119420.*

the fort. The surviving boats hurriedly reversed course and sailed back down the river and into the gulf, where transport ships waited in vain, never to participate in an invasion, because the mission was quickly in shambles.

The defeat at Sabine Pass seemingly underscored the importance of reducing the Confederate influence in the region to reassert the international interests of the Union. The second attempt to accomplish this objective proved to be much larger in scope. It involved nearly fifty thousand Union troops moving in a coordinated drive from both north and south to converge on Shreveport, Louisiana, located on the Red River less than twenty miles east of the Texas border.

Union strategists believed the occupation of Shreveport would ensure the eventual control of all Louisiana. In addition, the flow of valuable war matériel from Texas into Shreveport's warehouses would cease. Further, with the Trans-Mississippi rendered completely ineffective because of the Union occupation of Louisiana, tens of thousands of federal troops would be available for service in the more critical Eastern Theater. Moreover, and perhaps most important, there was cotton. To stop the export of Texas cotton would be to take from the Confederacy its principal trade commodity and to acquire the cotton already in Shreveport's warehouses would enhance the US Treasury by many millions of dollars.

It was clear to the War Department that with such a lucrative goal as Shreveport, a campaign of the magnitude as planned was definitely worthwhile. It was also equally clear to the Confederacy that every effort possible under the circumstances had to be made to repulse the Union's massive thrust up the Red River. The overall challenge of stopping the Union advance on Shreveport fell to Maj. Gen. Edmund Kirby Smith. Field command responsibilities and the twenty-five thousand-man Confederate force were divided equally between Lt. Gen. Richard Taylor and Maj. Gen. Sterling Price. The latter would remain in Arkansas to cripple any Union reinforcing movement intent on participating in the campaign.

Taylor, son of the hero of the Mexican War and later President of the United States, Zachary Taylor, was in command of the troops located in western Louisiana. Although he would have fewer than nine thousand men to halt the nearly forty thousand Union effectives moving up the Red River toward Shreveport, Taylor, every bit as aggressive and unorthodox as his famous father, sought to prove in combat that he was indeed his father's son in spirit as well as by blood.

General Banks, who aspired to a postwar political career he realized would benefit greatly from a major battlefield victory, commanded the Union forces on the march in Louisiana. He turned out to be as unpopular among his men, though, as Taylor was admired by his soldiers. The ten thousand men Banks borrowed from General William Tecumseh Sherman for the campaign seemed to be particularly dismissive of Banks' authoritarian style of leadership that had in large part contributed to his previous embarrassing performances as a commander in losing battles with Confederate Lt. Gen. Thomas J. (Stonewall) Jackson.

Almost as if to demonstrate his ineptitude in the field, Banks made a series of mistakes as he moved his huge force up the west side of the Red River in early April 1864. Although a key element of his advance entailed the covering support of a flotilla of thirty-five gunboats commanded by Adm. David Dixon Porter, Banks chose to use an interior stagecoach road for his northward progress rather than stay within the protective range of the naval guns. The route he chose was not only far less safe, but it was also less direct and passed through a heavily wooded area. At first, the sheer numbers of men in the Union advance compelled Taylor to retreat northward to within four miles of the roadway junction city of Mansfield. Reinforcements commanded by Brig. Gen. Thomas J. Churchill failed to arrive promptly enough for the fiery Taylor. Outnumbered at least two to one, Taylor determined to establish his lines of defense and force General Banks to do battle. Realizing the Union force was spread out along the stage road that Banks had foolishly chosen, and taking advantage of his enemy's failure to send out an effective number of advance scouts, Taylor awaited alongside the roadway with his troops concealed in the dense woods. He was ready to stop what later became known as the Union's unfortunate Red River Campaign.

The Battle

Around noon on April 8, Banks became aware of Taylor's presence before his advancing army marched into the crossfire trap. As Banks hurriedly placed his now twenty thousand-man force into battle lines, Taylor continued to wait, perhaps believing his tardy reinforcements would arrive in time to add strength to his limited force. Neither commander seemed particularly eager to commence the firefight, but when Confederate scouts observed Union infantry units moving forward with Banks' advance cavalry. Taylor swung into offensive action although the afternoon sun was already casting long shadows in the wooded area.

Brig. Gen Thomas Green, who commanded the Confederate cavalry at Mansfield, fought at San Jacinto in the War for Texas Independence twenty-eight years previously. On April 12, just four days after Mansfield, he died in action at Blair's Landing, Louisiana. General Green is buried in Austin's Oakwood Cemetery. Tom Green County, Texas, is named in honor of the general.

Early skirmishing accomplished little for either side, and Taylor, eager to mount a full attack against the still disorganized Union lines, ordered Brig. Gen. J. J. A. A. Mouton's division to strike the center of the federal position with Maj. Gen. John G. Walker on the left and Brig. Gen. William R. Scurry, of Glorieta battle fame, on the extreme right. The Confederate cavalry commanded by Brig. Gen. Thomas Green, another veteran of Brig. Gen. Henry Hopkins Sibley's ill-fated New Mexico Campaign, covered Taylor's flanks. At first, the Confederate charge halted when General Mouton was killed as he led his men across an open field. Overcoming a federal surge, Taylor's force succeeded when two of his divisions fought their way through the Union lines. The ensuing rout of the panic-stricken federal troops caused them to flee from the field. General Taylor quickly pursued the fleeing enemy, but his efforts to catch and annihilate what remained of Bank's army came to an end when General Kirby Smith ordered a halt, believing enough damage had been done as night fell across the battle scene. After the war, Taylor wrote that he thought Kirby Smith had been "incredibly stupid" to have halted his pursuit of Banks' shattered command.

The Battle of Mansfield nevertheless proved to be a major victory for the Confederacy. The Red River Campaign came to an unceremonious end there in western Louisiana. The failure of such an important campaign sponsored by President Lincoln was of such magnitude as to call for a federal congressional investigation that led to the relief from command of General Banks. Ironically, after the war, voters in his home state of Massachusetts elected him to Congress, the political body that had investigated his failure in Louisiana. He ultimately served six terms as a congressman.

The failure of the Red River Campaign prevented the Union from marching on Mobile, Alabama, which military leaders planned as the next step in the overall federal strategy. Further, Sherman's ten thousand men that he loaned for the campaign never returned to join him in his devastation of Georgia, whereas some fifteen thousand Confederate troops were now available to go to northwest Georgia to bolster the beleaguered troops fighting there to halt Sherman.

The battle at Mansfield was at least fleetingly important to the Southern cause. The Confederates suffered roughly one thousand casualties and the Union nearly twice that number. Once again, however, as was true with every battle from mid-1863 onward, the Confederates could not afford such losses, and although the Union grieved for the dead and those many wounded likely to die, there were many more men poised to take up arms in the North than in the South.

The Texans

In terms of percentage of all Confederate units engaged in the battle, those from Texas were in the majority at Mansfield. Those units were:

- 12th ("8th") Texas Infantry
- 18th Texas Infantry
- 22nd Texas Infantry
- 13th Texas Cavalry, Dismounted
- Haldeman's Texas Battery

All of Brig. Gen. Thomas N. Waul's Brigade, Walker's Division

- 11th Texas Infantry
- 14th Texas Infantry
- 6th (Gould's) Texas Cavalry Battalion, Dismounted
- 28th Texas Cavalry, Dismounted
- Daniel's Texas Battery

All of Brig. Gen. Horace Randal's Brigade, Walker's Division

- 15th Texas Infantry
- 17th Texas Consolidated Cavalry, Dismounted
- 22nd Texas Cavalry, Dismounted
- 31st Texas Cavalry, Dismounted
- 34th Texas Cavalry, Dismounted

All of Brig. Gen. Camille J. Polignac's Brigade, Mouton's Division

- Terrell's Texas Cavalry

All of Col. Augustus C. Buchel's Brigade, Bee's Division, Green's Cavalry Corps

- 1st Texas Infantry Regiments
- 2nd Texas Infantry Regiments

All of Col. Walter A. Lane's Brigade, Major's Division. Greens Cavalry Corps

- 4th Texas Cavalry
- 5th Texas Calvary
- 7th Texas Cavalry
- 13th (Walver's) Texas Cavalry Battalion

All of Brig. Gen. Arthur P. Bagby's Brigade, Major's Division. Green's Cavalry Corps

- Moseley's Nettles (Val Verde)
- Green's Cavalry Corps

The Monument

Of all the out-of-state Texas in the Civil War Monuments, the one with the closest ties to the Lone Star State in terms of proximity and the ultimate protection from invasion is the one dedicated in 1964 at the Mansfield State Historic Site in Louisiana. It is roughly twenty-five miles from the Texas state line and at the time must have seemed even closer to both residents of East Texas and those refugees fleeing before the advancing Union

Texas Gov. John Connally, a strong supporter of state programs to promote Texas history and tourism, poses with the Mansfield monument shortly before it was delivered to its battlefield location in Louisiana. *Courtesy of Texas Historical Commission.*

Army along the Red River. The closeness of the battlefield park also meant that it held the potential to benefit from Texas heritage tourists, and so the governments of both Louisiana and Texas worked closely to ensure the dedication ceremony would be special.

Early on the morning of April 4, 1964, people began to gather on the Shelby County Courthouse square in Center for what was officially billed as the Red River Civil War

Centennial Commemoration, or simply the Texas Muster. Following a program that included a pancake breakfast, speeches, special music by the Fairfield High School Band, a gun salute by the Rebel Guard of the Robert E. Lee High School in Tyler, and a rebel yell contest, participants in the day's events left town by 11:00 a.m. and traveled by auto caravan to Mansfield, where they first participated in a parade through the town at noon. Driving on to the park, four miles southeast, they gathered for dinner on the grounds. A full agenda program that included music, speeches by political figures, laying of wreaths, and more gun salutes and rebel yells began in earnest at 2:00. Among those speaking that day were Louisiana Gov. Jimmy Davis and Texas Lt. Gov. (later governor) Preston Smith. In his remarks, Smith noted, "We are not trying to refight the war but are striving to see that the true facts are fit into the proper perspective in our glorious history. . . . And that somehow—someway—we Texans will be worthy of the price paid for liberty—in victory and defeat. . . ." And so, he concluded, "one hundred years later—in Louisiana—bound to Texas with ties of blood—I dedicate this Confederate Memorial Information Marker in the name of and behalf of the State of Texas and order that it be unveiled in the sight and presence of God."

The Texas monument at Mansfield, the first in the series of out-of-state monuments, is unique because it is sited in front of the museum, which in turn is in the center of the historic battlefield at a point along the open ridge known as Honeycutt Hill near the Old Stage Road (Hwy. 175). To the west side is the location of the Confederate line from the first phase of the battle at 4:00 p.m., with the position of Polignac's Brigade to the north and Randal's Brigade and Waul's Brigade to the west. On the east side of the monument is the position of the federal battle line, with the closest units to the monument site at the time of battle being the 67th Indiana Volunteer Infantry, the 77th Illinois Volunteer Infantry, and Nim's Battery.

In recent years, Civil War enthusiasts and historical preservationists from Texas and Louisiana have worked together to check the advance of lignite mining in the area that threatens elements of the greater battlefield landscape along its eastern edge. There have also been joint state discussions regarding interstate regional tourism efforts that include the Mansfield State Historic Site.

Texans Remember

On the courthouse square in Bastrop, east of Austin, is a state historical monument for Joseph D. Sayers, wounded in action in the Battle of Mansfield. He returned to Confederate service and remained active through the war's end. After the war, he lived in Bastrop, from where he began a political career that included service as a US Congressman and as Texas governor. During his administration as the leader of the state, the first oil gusher blew in at Spindletop, marking what many believed to be the start of the modern era in Texas.

Another interesting state marker, located on the Shelby County Courthouse square, is for the Texas Muster of April 4, 1964, a defining moment in the state's historical preservation movement. The inscription reads in part:

Brig. Gen. William R. Scurry, who led the successful charge on the Union lines at Mansfield, was a veteran of the Mexican War. He was killed in action during the Battle of Jenkins' Ferry in Arkansas on April 30, 1864, three weeks following the Mansfield fight. Scurry County, Texas, is named in his honor. General Scurry is buried in the Texas State Cemetery in Austin.

Descendants answering to roll call for soldiers of 100 years ago included 37 sons and daughters of those fighters. Grandchildren, great-grandchildren and other kinsmen represented such leaders as the Trans-Mississippi commander, Gen. E. Kirby Smith, and Gens. A. P. Bagby, John R. Baylor, August Buchel, X. B. deBray, Tom Green, Walter P. Lane, Henry E. McCulloch, Jas. Major, Horace Randal, Wm. R. Scurry, Wm. Steele, John G. Walker, and Thos. Waul; and Cols. Henry Gray, Philip N. Luckett and P. C. Wood. Friends and descendants of the Val Verde Battery restored one century-old gun and brought it from Freestone County to ride in the 8-mile-long parade that moved 36 miles northeastward from here to the Mansfield Battleground. There the cannon shook the earth as it did April 8, 1864, and the assemblage unveiled the first out-of-state marker of the Texas Civil War Centennial, commemorating the Battle of Mansfield.

Directions to Monument

15149 Louisiana 175, southeast of Mansfield.

Suggested Readings

Ayres, Thomas. *Dark and Bloody Ground: The Battle of Mansfield and the Forgotten Civil War in Louisiana.* Lanham, MD: Taylor Trade Publishing, 2001.

Joiner, Gary Dillard. *One Damn Blunder from Beginning to End: The Red River Campaign of 1864.* Lanham, MD: Rowman and Littlefield, 2003.

————. *Through the Howling Wild: The 1864 Red River Campaign and Union Failure in the West.* Knoxville: University of Tennessee Press, 2003.

Johnson, Ludwell H. *Red River Campaign: Politics and Cotton in the Civil War.* Kent, OH: Kent State University Press, 1999. (Published 1958 by The Johns Hopkins University Press.)

TEXAS

REMEMBERS THE VALOR AND DEVOTION OF
HER SONS WHO SERVED AT THE WILDERNESS
MAY 6, 1864.

FROM NEAR THIS SPOT THE TEXAS BRIGADE
PLEADED WITH GENERAL LEE NOT TO
EXPOSE HIMSELF TO FEDERAL FIRE AND
THEN AFTER SEEING HIM TO SAFETY,
LAUNCHED A VIGOROUS COUNTERATTACK
THAT STEMMED THE ADVANCE OF HANCOCK'S
CORPS AND SAVED THE RIGHT FLANK OF
THE CONFEDERATE ARMY. OF APPROXIMATELY
800 TROOPS INVOLVED THE TEXAS BRIGADE
COUNTED OVER 500 CASUALTIES.

. . . .

A MEMORIAL TO TEXANS
WHO SERVED THE CONFEDERACY

ERECTED BY THE STATE OF TEXAS 1963

Battle of The Wilderness, Virginia

Also known as Combats at Parker's Stores, et al.

May 5–6, 1864

The Situation

By the time spring came to Virginia in 1864, the three-year-old Confederate States of America had only a slight chance to survive much longer. Its enemy's industrial strength was far greater than it had been at any time during the Civil War, and despite some concern about the expiration of many three-year enlistment contracts, its manpower was at least twice that of the Confederate Army. Although it is likely the very aggressive Gen. Robert E. Lee and a handful of his top lieutenants believed the survival of the Confederacy could still be assured only by winning a decisive battle, most politicians in Richmond saw the matter in a different light. To their more practical collective mind, the Confederacy could endure only if the North were to tire of the costly war and simply quit and let the South go its own way with its institution of slavery still intact. The most promising scenario that might have brought about such a solution would have been the defeat of Abraham Lincoln in the US presidential election of 1864. A peace candidate running on the Democratic Party's ticket might well have rallied the support of the hundreds of thousands of Northern voters believed to be yearning for the end of the savage fighting that had already taken the lives of so many young soldiers. With Lincoln and his cabinet out of power, the Southern leaders conjectured, the war would abruptly halt through an amicable agreement.

This scenario was not the exclusive property of the Richmond government. Lincoln himself was aware of what course a new administration might well take, and if that course were to lead to the recognition of the Confederacy and the resulting permanent dissolution of the Union he so dearly loved, Lincoln remained particularly motivated to stay in office. Lt. Gen. Ulysses S. Grant, the president's newly appointed general-in-chief of all Union armies, clearly shared Lincoln's desire to render at least part of the peace issue moot by crushing every Confederate army in the field to bring about the ultimate capitulation of the Confederacy itself months before the presidential election took place. To accomplish his task, Grant, with the enthusiastic endorsement of his commander-in-chief, put in motion a grand strategy designed to bring the already crippled Confederacy to its knees. In every theater of the war, Grant's generals set about aggressively attacking their enemies in a coordinated effort that would no longer make it possible for less embattled Southern units to be transferred to the aid of endangered forces engaged in hotly contested battles.

Trusting his lieutenants to fulfill his strategic plans in the other sectors, Grant posted himself in the headquarters of Maj. Gen. George Gordon Meade, there to oversee the relentless pursuit and eventual annihilation of General Lee and his still almost-mythic Army of Northern Virginia. Although Meade might likely have preferred Grant to go west to assist Maj. Gen. William Tecumseh Sherman in his fiery campaign against Gen. Joseph E. Johnston in Georgia, he recognized Lee was the most desirable quarry. To best him in a decisive battle would in all likelihood end the war, and even if it meant having Grant looking over his shoulder to do that, Meade became a grudgingly willing partner in the awkward arrangement.

As Grant saw it, he had to create every opportunity he could to draw Lee into battle. Then, taking advantage of his superiority in numbers (by a ratio of two to one), he had to defeat the wily Virginian as often as possible, all the while pushing him southward, ever closer to the Confederate capital at Richmond. The first step in Grant's plan to shatter the Army of Northern Virginia involved crossing the Rapidan River fifty-five miles north of Richmond, and only forty-five miles south of the federal capital at Washington. The route he chose was not only the most direct road to Richmond but also one that minimized the always lurking possibility of a daredevil Confederate raid on Washington itself. The route also provided a reliable thoroughfare for the long procession of wagons laden with the supplies so vital to the success of any invading army.

Despite the obvious attractiveness of Grant's chosen road to Richmond, there was one apparent negative aspect to it. After crossing the Rapidan, the large Union army would then be faced with the daunting challenge of making its ponderous way through an area aptly named The Wilderness. Located some ten miles west of Fredericksburg, Virginia, the heavily wooded tract was twelve miles wide and just over six miles deep, with its northern boundary being the south bank of the Rapidan River. General Meade was keenly aware of the inherent dangers involved in fighting in these woods, having done so some five months previously, only to be forced by the enemy to turn and flee back to the north, feeling fortunate to have survived. Grant, then, also obviously knew about the risks of doing battle in The Wilderness. Further, he knew Lee was already in those woods, at least partially entrenched and eagerly awaiting the arrival of Grant, Meade, and company. Despite everything he knew in advance, Grant decided to bull his way through the woods. He was in a hurry to move on to Richmond, and although he could have easily marched his army—or technically Meade's army—around this forbidding obstruction, Grant believed he would pass through it quickly before Lee could react to his speedy maneuver.

The trouble with Grant's plan was that he could not get his army to move *quickly* enough to surprise Lee. The Union's supply train could only make a slow southerly progress, and although Grant's 2,400 engineers made remarkable time in building pontoon bridges across the fords of the Rapidan, it still required much longer than foreseen for all of the wagons to cross those bridges. General Lee, who viewed The Wilderness as a useful ally in tempering the Union's superiority in manpower, intended to hit Grant from all sides as soon as he had crossed the Rapidan and entered the woods. The Union's delay in getting to the south bank of the river gave Lee the opportunity to seize the initiative in the battle that commenced around midday on May 5, 1864.

The Battle

The Union advance through the woods halted when troops in Maj. Gen. Gouvernor K. Warren's command encountered a small detachment of Confederate infantry moving toward them. The battle became fully joined in the early afternoon when two of Lee's corps faced off against three Union corps moving south. The initial engagement came about earlier than Lee had planned despite the fact that the frequently slow-moving command of Lt. Gen. James Longstreet did not arrive on schedule.

The first day of the battle ended without either side accomplishing much more than stumbling about in the nearly impenetrable bramble-choked woods. Even though Grant had some 115,000 soldiers to commit to the firefight versus Lee's 64,000, the Southerners knew the terrain. If any locations could be found in the trees to place artillery, the Confederates would be the first to find them, even though the density of the woods minimized the potential effectiveness of any sustained barrage by either side.

The second day began with a strong Union attack that pushed the Confederates back to one of the rare open fields to be found in the woods. General Lee had placed his headquarters in the clearing, a quickly discovered fact warmly received by the hard-charging Union men. What happened next became the stuff of long-lived Texas legend. Seeing their beloved commander directly in the path of the federal onslaught, Brig. Gen. John Gregg's Texans rushed to his defense. Recognizing his would-be saviors as Texans, Lee saluted them with great enthusiasm and then, caught up in the fever of battle, set out to lead Gregg's men in a counterattack himself. Fearing for his life, the Texans demanded Lee go back to the rear where all such particularly revered commanding generals rightfully belonged. Vowing not to move forward until Lee moved rearward, the men from Texas finally persuaded Lee to give up his temporary role as a brigade commander in the field. Reportedly, it was not until a Texas sergeant seized the reins of Lee's horse and turned it away from the fighting that the general halted his personal assault on Grant's army.

Brig. Gen. John Gregg, commander of the Texas Brigade in The Wilderness fight, was a former resident of Fairfield, Texas, and a one-time district judge. He was killed in action below Richmond on October 7, 1864.

The counterattack, thus inspired, served to stop the Union advance. From that point on, and until the Confederates were able to flank Grant's invading force to eventually carry the day and then the battle itself, the fighting deteriorated into a veritable hell of brush fires, blinding smoke, confused and usually leaderless isolated sorties, and countless instances of friendly fire killing or wounding men wearing identical uniforms. One of the victims of such unintentional shooting was General Longstreet himself, painfully wounded by one of his own soldiers who fired at a figure through the dense smoke only to discover later it was his general who had been hit. Longstreet survived his wounding, although he was out of action for nearly half of a very critical year.

One report had it that upon discovering his forces flanked and his plan to dash through The Wilderness thwarted, Grant went to his tent and wept. True or not, any such temporary breakdown did not long hinder the fighting spirit of Lincoln's new general-in-chief. He promptly led his men back out of the woods away from the fire and away from the canny Lee, who had somehow wrested a tactical victory out of the fiery chaos of The Wilderness. Once again, it appeared a Union juggernaut superior in both men and arms stood poised to slink away in defeat, its forward onslaught halted by a smaller but apparently more dedicated Confederate force. What appeared to be the case, however, quickly proved to be a false perception. Once out of the woods, Grant at first surprised and then delighted his men by not slipping away northward to the safety of Washington's strong defensive positions, but rather by turning south toward Richmond seeking yet another chance to crush Lee's Army of Northern Virginia. Of the 116,000 men Grant had led into The Wilderness, an astounding 18,000 became casualties of the fight. Lee's 60,000-man force lost nearly 11,000, but he had carried the battle.

The Texans who urged Gen. Robert E Lee to "go back" during the battle came into The Wilderness eight hundred strong. More than half of them were killed or wounded during the fighting on May 6, 1864.

Long after the war ended, many generals and even a greater number of theorizing historians saw fit to point out exactly where and when the Confederacy began to lose its fight for independence. Some put it at Corinth, others at Vicksburg, and far more put it at Gettysburg, but it is perhaps more than likely the Confederacy's ultimate failure became sealed the moment Grant turned south on May 6, 1864. Although Grant had lost a tactical battle to Lee, he attained what proved to be a strategic victory after all. Lee was soon reduced to fighting what essentially was a rear guard action that eventually led him to Appomattox Court House and the surrender of his Army of Northern Virginia. That it required nearly another year to bring Lee, the "Gray Fox," to bay is a bloody testament both to his stubborn resolve and zealous love of his state. It is also an even bloodier testament to Grant's relentlessness and willingness to sacrifice however many lives it took to overtake and bring down his Confederate prey. In truth, it all really began to end for the Confederacy while the smoke still continued to rise from the shattered wasteland of The Wilderness.

The Texans

General Gregg's Texas Brigade, long associated with Brig. Gen. John Bell Hood, was famously present at the battle of The Wilderness. Included in the brigade were:
- 1st Texas Infantry Regiment, Lt. Col. F. S. Bass commanding
- 4th Texas Infantry Regiment, Col. J. P. Bane commanding
- 5th Texas Infantry Regiment, Lt. Col. K. Bryan commanding

General Gregg's Brigade was part of Maj. Gen. Charles W. Field's Division, Lt. Gen. James Longstreet's Corps.

The Monument

The Texas Civil War Monument on The Wilderness Battlefield is unique because of the inscriptions incised on the back panel. Whereas other monuments in the series have additional information on the backside, most of that space is reserved for lists of participating units. At The Wilderness, however, visitors find reference to a poignant battlefield scene, the words attributed to the noted historian and Lee biographer, Douglas Southall Freeman:

> "Who are you, my boys?" Lee cried as he saw them gathering.
> "Texas boys," they yelled, their number multiplying every second.
> The Texans—Hood's Texans of Longstreet's Corps, just at the right place and at the right moment! After the strain of the dawn, the sight of these grenadier guards of the South was too much for Lee. For once the dignity of the commanding general was shattered; for once his poise was shaken.
> "Hurrah for Texas," he shouted, waving his hat: "Hurrah for Texas."
> . . . the willing veterans sprang into position. . . he would lead them in the countercharge . . . he spurred. . . Traveller. . . on the heels of the infantry men.
> . . . "Go back, General Lee, go back!" they cried. . . "We won't go on unless you go back!"

In identifying an adoptive sponsor for restoration of the monument, the Texas Historical Commission (THC) was fortunate to receive assistance from Janet Jacobs, preservation chair of the Friends of the Wilderness Battlefield. Through her efforts, the Pelath family of Fredericksburg, Virginia, stepped forward to take on the project. In a 1999 note to the THC staff, Sherry Pelath wrote:

Using detailed information and specifications provided by the Texas Historical Commission, and working in association with the Friends of the Wilderness Battlefield, members of the Pelath family of Virginia took on the restoration of the Texas monument. *Courtesy of Texas Historical Commission.*

> When I first read of the need for a volunteer to restore the Texas Monument. . . I was motivated to respond for three reasons. First of all, we are from Austin, Texas; the monument, being made of pink granite, made us feel closer to home. Secondly, my favorite person in American History is General Robert E. Lee, and the Texans for whom this monument is dedicated saved General Lee's life by refusing to move forward into battle until he removed himself to the rear. When they knew their General was safe, these same courageous Texans went into a fierce battle that decimated their ranks. Third, this battle was on May 6th which was my birthday.

She concluded by noting, "I just want to say that restoring the Texas Monument was, for me, a labor of love."

Texans Remember
When the survey team from the THC made its inspection of the state monument at The Wilderness in the late 1990s, it found fresh flowers and a small Texas flag placed at the site, a reminder that the memories of those who served on the battlefield still resonate with current generations.

Members of the Pelath family, former residents of Texas, pose beside the restored monument in 1999. *Courtesy of Texas Historical Commission.*

Directions to Monument

Widow Trapp Farm section of the Fredericksburg and Spotsylvania National Military Park. Route 621 south of Locust Grove. For detailed information, inquire at park visitor center, 120 Chatham Road, Fredericksburg.

Suggested Readings

Gallagher, Gary W., ed. *The Wilderness Campaign.* Chapel Hill: University of North Carolina Press, 1997.

McWhiney, Grady. *Battle in the Wilderness: Grant Meets Lee.* Austin: State House Press, 1998.

Rhea, Gordon C. *The Battle of the Wilderness, May 5–6, 1864.* Baton Rouge: Louisiana State University Press, 1994.

TEXAS
REMEMBERS THE VALOR AND DEVOTION OF
HER SONS WHO SERVED AT CHEATHAM HILL
KENNESAW MOUNTAIN AND IN OTHER
ENGAGEMENTS OF THE ATLANTA CAMPAIGN IN
1864.

. . . .

A MEMORIAL TO TEXANS
WHO SERVED THE CONFEDERACY

ERECTED BY THE STATE OF TEXAS 1964

Battle of Kennesaw Mountain, Georgia

June 27, 1864

The Situation

As Lt. Gen. Ulysses S. Grant moved inexorably against Gen. Robert E. Lee and toward his strategic goal of Richmond, Virginia, his chief lieutenant conducted a simultaneous and almost identical campaign in the West. Maj. Gen. William Tecumseh Sherman's advance toward his initial goal of Atlanta, Georgia, involving a continuous series of strikes against Gen. Joseph E. Johnston, proved to be a mirror image of Grant's actions in Virginia. In the Georgia Campaign, however, Sherman discovered that the obstacles blocking his road to Atlanta were a series of well-defended sites made even more formidable by their natural setting in forests or on rugged hilltops. As was true with Grant's advance, Sherman faced major logistical problems that challenged any invading army. The fact that the Georgians his men encountered along their way were not at all inclined to voluntarily aid and abet or feed their invaders only served to exacerbate the Union's supply problem.

Sherman's force consisted of three distinct Union armies with a collective total manpower of more than 100,000. The largest of these armies was Maj. Gen. George H. Thomas's Army of the Cumberland, with 60,000 men; James B. McPherson's Army of the Tennessee included some 30,000. The smallest of the units, The Army of the Ohio, commanded by Maj. Gen. John M. Schofield, had 14,000 names on its roster.

The magnitude of the supply requirements of such a massive force is reflected in the logistical statistics shown in the three armies' combined field report. More than five thousand heavily laden wagons trailed behind the marching men, and a giant remuda of forty thousand horses ensured enough fresh horsepower to pull the wagons to their destination. General Johnston, fighting an admirable delaying action against such a mammoth and determined foe, had only forty thousand men with which to inflict any telling damage to Sherman's invaders. Johnston and his fellow generals, William J. Hardee and John Bell Hood, his chief subordinate, did however have the singular advantages of knowing the terrain and being able to fight from well-fortified positions. General Sherman himself once concluded that one man in a trench was the equivalent of three to four men charging that trench. Further, the trees and thick brush that lay along Sherman's march provided effective cover for Confederate snipers and sharpshooters, each deadly accurate because of their largely rural upbringing that placed high value on keen marksmanship.

Despite the few advantages held by the Confederates, Sherman's progress toward Atlanta could at best only be retarded but never brought fully to a halt. Efforts to do so at Rocky Face Ridge, Resaca, New Hope Church, Kolb's Farm, and other engagements had been costly to both sides, but after each encounter General Johnston could only manage to pull back to another readily defended point toward which Sherman marched with minimal delay but with growing frustration. The fiery Union commander was apparently as competitive as he was relentless. According to some accounts, he chafed at the resourcefulness being shown by General Johnston in finding both the ways and the means to so impressively delay the Yankee juggernaut. An admirer of the Confederate leader who was keeping him away from Atlanta, Sherman made note that every time his men overpowered one of Johnston's defensive strongholds, another one could arise from the red Georgia soil. The enemy's network of trenches, Sherman complained, seemed to be at least fifty miles long, each connected to another.

Confederate General Joseph E. Johnston, Maj. Gen. William Tecumseh Sherman's principal adversary during the final months of the Civil War, served as a pallbearer at the Union general's funeral in February 1891. He caught a chill in the rainy procession and died five weeks later of pneumonia.

Newspaper accounts of Grant's victories in Virginia, bloody though they were, fueled Sherman's frustrations further. His senior commander's apparent relative success in driving Lee down to Richmond rendered his own tedious skirmish-by-skirmish advance toward Atlanta somewhat pale in comparison. When an article strongly hinted that perhaps Sherman was not truly a fighter, at least in the relentless Grant-like sense of the term, it was just a matter of time until Sherman's maneuvering against Johnston had to cease in favor of a decisive battle that would hush his critics.

Backpedaling from three Union armies and a commander who was more than enough of a fighter for his tastes, General Johnston seems to have shared his opponent's frustration at the hit-and-run nature Sherman's campaign had assumed. His men were weary of being continuously in retreat just as were Sherman's men equally weary of having to maneuver and skirmish rather than hit their enemy with all of the superior armed might at their disposal.

The Northern press called for a clear-cut victory from Sherman just as Southern newspapers, along with the Confederacy's leadership, demanded that Johnston be more aggressive in crippling and perhaps permanently halting the Union advance. On June 27, 1864, on the rough terrain of Kennesaw Mountain, both commanders would have an opportunity to satisfy the many demands being made upon them by the press and by their political leaders.

The Battle

Kennesaw Mountain has an elevation of slightly less than seven hundred feet, towering over the surrounding terrain. It provided a likely spot for the long-simmering need for a mutually desired decisive battle to take place. At the mountain's base curved the tracks of the strategically vital Western & Atlantic Railway. To gain control of that railway system would be to alleviate Sherman's ever-increasing problem of supply. Just beyond the mountain to the east lay the town of Marietta, an important transportation and logistical center. Even though he was well aware of the extraordinary strength of the Confederate defensive lines in front of and on the summit of the mountain, Sherman clearly felt compelled, for military and perhaps even personal reasons, to assault it in a frontal attack. Johnston, on the other hand, reasoned that if Sherman were foolish or hardheaded enough to hurl his men against those defenses, a Union failure would equate to a Confederate victory. Then, at least maybe, the pressure flowing out of Richmond upon him might perhaps be diminished.

In planning his assault, Sherman sought to outsmart his adversary as well as substantially outnumber him. Although the Confederate flanks were possibly weaker, the Union general decided to attack the Confederate center, where he assumed the enemy would not expect such a direct frontal assault. The Union's preliminary probes confirmed that the enemy's flanks were even more stoutly defended than previous reconnaissance had indicated. As a result, Sherman became convinced that the center was the best place to crash through the lines and take the mountain, impregnable though it might seem to a less-aggressive commander. To enhance the odds for success in what might be something of a suicidal mission, he kept his plan secret from all but his most immediate lieutenants. The highly classified plan called for a massive artillery barrage of exactly one hour's duration to hopefully clear the intended path of the assault of all, or at least nearly all, impediments to the soldiers' progress up the mountainsides. Following the barrage, at exactly 8:00 a.m. on June 27, 1864, the Union horde would then storm the assumedly shattered defenses and sweep up the slope to an easy victory.

Apparently Sherman's demand for secrecy to shroud his plan of attack prevailed. However, the lengthy barrage by his 250 field pieces did give the defenders a noisy hint that Union forces would likely be coming up the mountain just as soon as the overheated guns fell silent. Sherman's assumptions about the attack were only partly valid. He believed his men were far more eager to fight than to continue the less than glamorous work of maneuvering. He also believed his lines were, at least for the moment, as extended as they could safely be. Right as he was on those two aspects, Sherman was dead wrong in his assumption that the

A private of the 6th Texas Infantry, one of the units that participated in the intense fighting at Kennesaw Mountain, Georgia. *Courtesy of Library of Congress, AMB/TIN no. 2855 [P&P].*

Confederate defenses were much weaker than indicated. Further, his hopes that an hour's worth of heavy shelling could render whatever defenses actually existed completely harmless were quickly dashed. Less than two hours after it began, the Union assault crumpled. High temperatures, a tough terrain that formed natural defenses, and the withering fire that poured down upon the attackers brought federal charges and even more charges to a standstill, although often only a few paces from the Confederate lines. The Union managed to break through the first of those lines, but vicious hand-to-hand combat forced them to hurriedly withdraw.

During the course of the roughly 105-minute fight, fires broke out in the dense woods and undergrowth that so effectively hindered the Union attack. Just as had been the case during the Battle of the Wilderness over in General Grant's sector, the flames caused by artillery and rifle fire soon scorched the bodies of many of the Union men wounded in the assault. In one of those priceless and all-too-rare instances of an act of humanity performed in heated combat, a Confederate colonel called out to the retreating attackers that a cease-fire was in effect to permit the wounded to be carried to safety beyond the reach of the fires. Reportedly, soldiers on both sides of the fray worked together under a white flag of truce to clear the burning woods of fallen Union soldiers. As a reward for his gallantry, so the story goes, a grateful Union officer presented the lifesaving Confederate colonel with a valuable set of pearl-handled pistols after the battle.

All such gallantry aside, neither side gained much in the Battle of Kennesaw Mountain. The Union suffered roughly 3,000 casualties and the Confederates losses were slightly more than 750. If anything useful came from the fight that might in part justify the losses incurred, it could be that General Sherman learned, or at least recalled from his previous similar experiences, that to attack a deeply entrenched enemy is a costly and largely futile endeavor. General Johnston, on the other hand, recalled that no matter how formidable the defenses, a massive enemy force can only be delayed in its progress and not decisively defeated nor permanently discouraged from pressing onward.

In a short time, Sherman did press on, through Marietta, through Atlanta, and on to the Atlantic Ocean. His failure to stem that progress soon cost General Johnston his command, but only for a time. Unlike with many battles in the Civil War, few historians have ever claimed that the fight at Kennesaw Mountain in any way determined the eventual outcome of the war itself. It was at best just another bloody delaying action along the road to the downfall of the Confederacy, which came about less than a year later.

Among the Union forces serving at Kennesaw Mountain was a soldier of the Ohio 35th Volunteer Infantry named Abraham Landis. He later had a son he named for the battle, using a variant of the spelling. Kenesaw Mountain Landis became a respected jurist and later the first commissioner of Major League Baseball.

The Texans

Texas units participating in the Battle of Kennesaw Mountain and other engagements of the Georgia Campaign were:

- 6th Texas Infantry Regiment
- 15th Texas Cavalry, Dismounted, Capt. Rhoads Fisher commanding
- 7th Texas Infantry Regiment, Capt. J. H. Collett commanding
- 10th Texas Infantry Regiment, Col. Roger Q. Mills commanding
- 17th Texas Cavalry, Dismounted, Capt. George D. Manion commanding
- 18th Texas Cavalry, Dismounted, Capt. George D. Manion commanding
- 24th Texas Cavalry, Dismounted, Col. Franklin C. Wilkes commanding
- 25th Texas Cavalry, Dismounted, Col. Franklin C. Wilkes commanding

All were part of Cleburne's Division, Brig. Gen. Hiram B. Granbury's and Brig. Gen. J. A. Smith's Brigade.

The Monument

The Texas Civil War Monument is located where state forces served in the vicinity of Cheatham Hill, the scene of the fiercest fighting of the battle. It was along the Confederate lines at Cheatham Hill where Union units unleashed the brunt of their massive and seemingly relentless assault, but thanks to valiant fighting by many Southern units, including those from Texas, the Confederate line held firm against overwhelming odds. The monument at Kennesaw Mountain was among the first approved by the Texas Civil War Centennial Commission, and the Texas State Historical Survey Committee (TSHSC) sought and received formal approval for the site within the National Park. Approval came via longtime park superintendent, Bowling Cox Yates, the ideal person to shepherd the request. First hired as a historian at the site in the 1930s through Civil Works Administration funds during the New Deal Era, Yates began his work at Kennesaw Mountain National Battlefield Park by developing an interpretive plan for the Cheatham Hill area. In his June 17, 1963, letter to TSHSC director George Hill, he noted, "the Regional Director, Southeast Region, National Park Service, has advised me today that it is satisfactory for you to proceed with the erection of the Texas Monument," but then added without explanation, "omitting the quotation formerly proposed for inscription." Just what that quotation was and why it did not meet with National Park Service (NPS) approval is unknown. With the letter, though, Yates included maps showing two approved monument locations, including the one the state ultimately selected.

Texans Remember

An Official Texas Historical Marker (100 W. Houston) in the North Texas town of Sherman commemorates the service of the 11th Texas Cavalry for the Confederacy. Initially organized in May 1861 as a frontier unit under the command of Col. William C. Young, it participated in successful military operations in the Indian Territory (present-day Oklahoma) before induction into Confederate service and subsequent action in Arkansas. Following the Battle of Elkhorn Tavern it, like many other early Southern cavalry units in the early days of the war, became essentially an infantry, or cavalry dismounted, regiment (11th Texas Cavalry, Dismounted) for a time. Reinstated as a cavalry in 1863 following fighting at Murfreesboro, Tennessee, it remained a particularly active unit throughout the war. The 11th Texas served with distinction in such key battles as Chickamauga, Kennesaw Mountain, and Bentonville.

Irish-born Maj. Gen. Patrick Cleburne was a promising young field commander beloved by his troops and considered by many to be the "Stonewall Jackson of the West." He died in the Battle of Franklin, Tennessee, one of six generals killed in that conflict. *Courtesy of Library of Congress, LC-USZ-107446.*

Directions to Monument

Cheatham Hill Drive, south of Whitlock Avenue NW (Dallas Highway), west of Marietta in the Kennesaw Mountain National Battlefield Park. For additional information, inquire at the park visitor center, 900 Kennesaw Mountain Drive, Kennesaw.

Suggested Readings

Baumgartner, Richard A., and Larry M. Strayer. *Kennesaw Mountain, June 1864: Bitter Standoff at the Gibraltar of Georgia.* Huntington, WV: Blue Acorn Press, 1998.

Blount, Russell W., Jr. *Clash at Kennesaw, June and July, 1864.* Gretna, LA: Pelican Press, 2012.

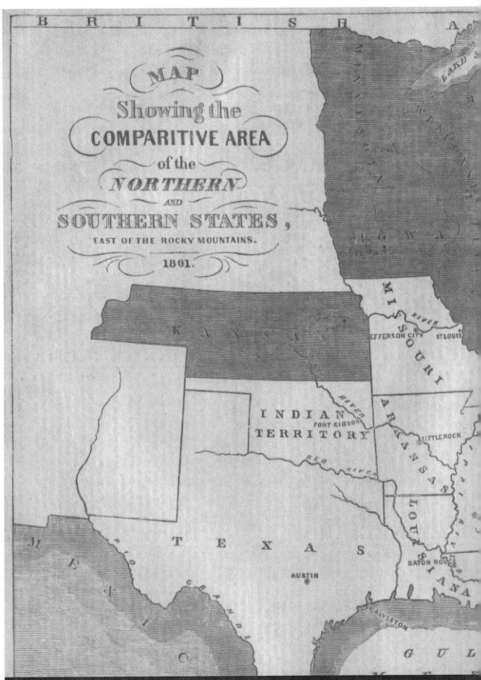

MAP
Showing the
COMPARITIVE AREA
of the
NORTHERN
AND
SOUTHERN STATES,
EAST OF THE ROCKY MOUNTAINS.
1861.

The march of Sherman's army from Atlanta to the sea and north to Golds
. . . was magnificent in its results, also equally magnificent in the way it
conducted. —*Ulysses S. Grant*

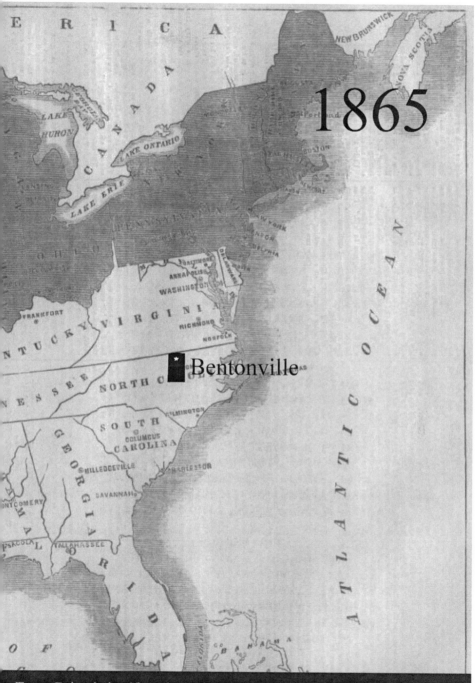

1865

Bentonville

he Texas Brigade itself, perhaps the most renowned of all, 476 officers and marched up the road, and stacked the rifles that had been heard in all the Army's great battles. . . . —*Douglas Southall Freeman*

TEXAS
REMEMBERS THE VALOR AND DEVOTION
OF HER SONS WHO SERVED AT BENTONVILLE
MARCH 19-21, 1865.

THE EIGHTH TEXAS CAVALRY WAS ENGAGED
WITH THE LEFT WING OF SHERMAN'S UNION
ARMY ON THE EVE OF THE BATTLE OF
BENTONVILLE. DURING THE BATTLE ON
MARCH 21, THE EIGHTH TEXAS AGAIN
PERFORMED VALUABLE SERVICE IN THE
CONFEDERATE ATTACK ON UNION GENERAL
JOSEPH MOWER'S DIVISION OF THE
SEVENTEENTH ARMY CORPS. LIEUTENANT-
GENERAL WILLIAM J. HARDEE, COMMANDING
A CORPS IN THE BATTLE, ORDERED ABOUT
80 MEN OF THE EIGHTH TEXAS COMMANDED
BY CAPTAIN "DOC" MATHEWS, A MERE BOY,
TO OPPOSE MOWER'S ADVANCE. THE TEXANS
ATTACKED IN CONJUNCTION WITH OTHER
CAVALRY COMMANDED BY GENERAL WHEELER
AND LIEUTENANT-GENERAL WADE HAMPTON
AND CUMMING'S GEORGIA BRIGADE. YOUNG
"WILLIE" HARDEE, GENERAL HARDEE'S ONLY
SON, CHARGED WITH THE EIGHTH TEXAS AND
WAS KILLED. UNDER HEAVY CONFEDERATE
PRESSURE, MOWER SOON WITHDREW HIS
DIVISION TO ITS ORIGINAL POSITION.
DURING THE CONFEDERATE RETREAT FROM
BENTONVILLE THE EIGHTH AND ELEVENTH
TEXAS CAVALRY PLAYED A PROMINENT ROLE

(REVERSE SIDE)
IN OPPOSING THE UNION PURSUIT FROM
MILL CREEK BRIDGE UNTIL THE PURSUERS
WITHDREW AT HANNAH'S CREEK. THE TEXANS
WERE SURRENDERED WITH THE REMNANTS
OF THE ARMY OF TENNESSEE AT GREENSBORO
NORTH CAROLINA IN MAY 1865

. . . .

A MEMORIAL TO TEXANS
WHO SERVED THE CONFEDERACY
ERECTED BY THE STATE OF TEXAS 1964

Battle of Bentonville,
North Carolina

March 19–21, 1865

The Situation

Although Confederate Gen. Joseph E. Johnston's strong defensive tactics at Kennesaw Mountain delayed Maj. Gen. William Tecumseh Sherman's conquest of Atlanta, it did not prevent that statistically inevitable event from occurring just months later. The Union occupation of Georgia's largest and most important city on September 2, 1864, had a more telling impact on the future of the Confederacy than many of the Civil War's previous engagements. As the war progressed into its third and then its fourth year, the sheer military and industrial might of the North made it increasingly apparent to most Confederate leaders, with the notable exception of the new nation's president, that their dreams of independence were likely soon to be dashed. The only flickering light remaining at the end of the war's dark and bloody tunnel was that enough Northern voters would express their displeasure with the duration and cost of the war to remove US President Abraham Lincoln from power in Washington, DC. Lincoln's Democratic Party opponent in the November 1864 presidential election was someone few Southerners would have endorsed in the early years of the war: retired Union Gen. George B. McClellan, the onetime would-be conqueror of Richmond and the nominal victor over Gen. Robert E. Lee at Sharpsburg.

Before Atlanta fell, there was genuine reason to believe Lincoln's war was more than unpopular with enough Northerners to cause them to cast a majority vote for McClellan. Lincoln himself apparently believed that his onetime general-in-chief, who now vigorously denounced both the president and his war, appeared likely to win at the polls. When Atlanta fell, however, just two months before the election, Lincoln received the prize he needed to demonstrate to the electorate that the war was at last in its final stages. McClellan was above all else a professional soldier, albeit a forcibly retired one, and as such he could not in good conscience continue to deride the now-obvious success attained by General Sherman in Georgia. That success deprived him of the most significant plank in his platform. When Atlanta fell to Sherman's soldiers, McClellan lost whatever chance he had to become president of the United States.

Confederate President Jefferson Davis was foremost among the few Southerners who never believed Lincoln would lose the election in 1864. Davis's character was so entwined with the Confederate cause it is possible he also seriously doubted that a victorious McClellan, once president, would have actually negotiated with him to allow the Confederacy to go its own way, unchallenged and forever free of the perceived federal yoke. Less than a month after the occupation of Atlanta, President Davis still made fiery speeches claiming Confederate forces would soon crush Sherman and send him reeling out of Georgia in total defeat.

General Sherman, on the other hand, made few public speeches, intent instead on making plans to essentially destroy Georgia by total warfare and not at all to be sent reeling from it in defeat. At first, Sherman's newly appointed general-in-chief and close friend, Lt. Gen. Ulysses S. Grant, had other plans for Sherman's army now that Atlanta was in federal hands. With Lee being relentlessly pushed back toward the Confederate capital by Grant's massive army, he ordered Sherman to hurry northward through the Carolinas to attack Lee's Army of Northern Virginia from its rear, thus to successfully end the war at last. Sherman, of course, eventually acceded to the orders of his superior officer. After pursuing Gen. John Bell Hood's failed but still dangerous army in its flight from the smoldering ruin that had been Atlanta, however, Sherman initially tuned south, intent on marching to the sea before then marching to join Grant in Virginia. On his way to Savannah on Georgia's Atlantic coast, he vowed to make the state and its ravaged citizens "howl" by employing his unique brand of brutal total warfare. The general's vow soon came to pass.

As Sherman marched through Georgia, his defeated adversary during the Battle of Atlanta continued his march to the west, hoping somehow, to reach General Lee in time to halt Grant's inexorable thrust toward Richmond. General Hood, having been placed in command of the Army of Tennessee by President Davis in relief of General Johnston, soon met defeat at the hands of Union General George H. Thomas at the Battle of Franklin on November 30, 1864. His army all but destroyed, Hood requested his own removal from command and became inactive until the end of the war some five months later.

In the meantime, the already beleaguered General Lee had been given command of all Confederate armies by President Davis, who still envisioned some sort of military miracle in the field would halt the rampaging Union armies now within cannon range of victory on nearly all fronts. With Hood voluntarily out of command, the Confederate army desperately needed a new general to lead the once powerful Army of Tennessee. Lee's choice for the job was none other than Johnston, the very general that President Davis had relieved of the same command after Johnston's failure to halt Sherman's advance toward Atlanta. Davis had never been keen on the newly appointed general's ability to win battles, but Lee's persuasion and the absence of any other viable candidate gave him little choice but to agree to the reassignment of Johnston.

The fifty-eight-year-old Johnston attempted to make the most of what he must surely have realized would be his last opportunity to best Sherman on the field. When he learned that his antagonist was moving rapidly into North Carolina on his way to join Grant following his particularly harsh demonstration of total war in South Carolina, General Johnston saw his opportunity and he seized it.

The Battle

General Sherman's immediate goal in North Carolina was the city of Goldsborough (now Goldsboro), there to consolidate his scattered forces to make any further Confederate resistance pointless. Sherman marched through North Carolina without any significant opposition and with an almost complete absence of the total war horrors he had inflicted upon Georgia, and particularly upon South Carolina. Sherman's men, remembering well that South Carolina was the first to secede from the Union, ravaged the state with a particular vengeance.

The Union advance toward Goldsborough moved forward in two columns. Aware of this separation of forces, Johnston set a trap that would surprise and hopefully annihilate the column making up the left wing of the advance. Although he had only seventeen thousand men to spring his trap, Johnston did have a large and talented senior officer corps that warranted a command many times larger. In addition to himself, there were Braxton Bragg, also a full general, plus three lieutenant generals and five major generals, all of whom seemed to be cooperating to an unusual degree in the last ditch effort to derail the Sherman express before it teamed up with Grant for what would clearly be the final blow to the Confederate cause. On March 19, 1865, Sherman's left wing walked into the ambush. At first, the trap had some success, but in time the Union men managed to blunt the Confederate surprise attack. For the next two days, the two sides skirmished to little lasting effect.

On March 21, the right wing of Sherman's sixty thousand-man force arrived to take up a position within yards of the beleaguered left wing, still trading shots with the enemy. An unplanned counterattack by Bvt. Maj. Gen. Joseph A. Mower's XVII Corps forced the Confederates back to General Johnston's headquarters, causing him to hastily retreat along with his entire staff. Yet another counterattack, this time led by Confederate Lt. Gen. William J. Hardee, halted Mower's advance and forced the Union men well back along the road. At this juncture, and for some unknown reason, the usually aggressive General Sherman broke off the day's fighting. The next day, Johnston chose to retreat from the field, and for a time Sherman's men pursued them. Not unlike a gigantic cat toying with a weakened mouse, the Union general abandoned the pursuit after a short time and let Johnston slip away.

Although he led the last major Confederate offensive action of the Civil War, Johnston was realist enough to know that it had been in vain. On April 18, 1865, after learning Grant's pursuit of Lee had successfully ended at Appomattox Court House, Virginia, the weary Johnston began negotiating with Sherman about terms of surrender. The Union general, far more benevolent in victory than when fighting to attain it, gave Johnston terms considered much too favorable by Washington authorities. The parties reached a revised settlement on April 26, 1865, despite the initially heated opposition of President Davis, who apparently still believed his devoutly desired military miracle would yet come to pass and wash away the now undeniable pain of obvious defeat. That miracle never came, of course. There were just not enough men left to create any such miraculous occurrence. When Johnston's thirty thousand men laid down their arms at Raleigh, North Carolina, on May 2, 1865, the Confederate cause drew its final enfeebled breath. America's great Civil War was over.

> Willie Hardee, the sixteen-year old son of Confederate Lt. Gen. William J. Hardee, had long begged his father for permission to don a uniform to fight with the famed Texas 8th Cavalry. At the Battle of Bentonville, young Hardee got his wish, only to die instantly in a counterattack initiated by his father.

The Texans

The following Texas units participated at the Battle of Bentonville.

- 6th Texas Infantry Regiment
- 7th Texas Infantry Regiment
- 10th Texas Infantry Regiment
- 15th Texas Infantry Regiment

Each was part of Granbury's Brigade, Cleburne's Division, Johnston's Corps

- 17th Texas Cavalry, Dismounted
- 18th Texas Cavalry, Dismounted
- 24th Texas Cavalry, Dismounted
- 25th Texas Cavalry, Dismounted
- 8th Texas Cavalry
- 11th Texas Cavalry

All part of Harrison's Brigade, Hume's Division, Wheeler's Cavalry Corps, Hampton's Cavalry Command

The Monument

The Texas Civil War Monument is located in the Bentonville Battlefield State Historic Site near the Harper House along Harper House Road, Four Oaks, North Carolina. The Harper House was a battlefield landmark and served as a field hospital. The site represents only a small portion of the original battlefield, which spread more than six thousand acres, so the monument is commemorative in nature. It is important, though, that it is sited near a monument for North Carolina troops.

When the Texas Historical Commission (THC) survey team visited the site in September 1998, it found the text of the Texas monument completely illegible, with no trace of original paint in the letters. As a result, frustrated heritage tourists had even taken to rubbing dirt or mud in the incised areas so they could be read. Through a cooperative agreement between the THC and park staff, along with assistance from the Bentonville Battleground Historical Association, volunteers worked to restore the legibility of the text. The Bentonville monument is unique in

Brig. Gen. William J. Hardee, a veteran of the Mexican War, commanded Texas forces at Bentonville and lost his teenage son in the battle. *Courtesy of Library of Congress, LOT 4213 [item] [P&P].*

that it not only has text on both sides, but a star and wreath on both sides as well.

Texans Remember

Two Official Texas Historical Markers in Hardin County in Southeast Texas commemorate the life of North Carolina native Gen. Braxton Bragg. One, located on the courthouse square in Kountze, notes that Bragg moved to Galveston, Texas, in the early 1870s and worked as chief engineer of the Gulf, Colorado, & Santa Fe Railway then building a line across the state. As crews surveyed the route through Hardin County, company officials named a junction point for the former general. The town of Bragg remained in existence until the 1930s, serving as a supply and operations point for the nearby Saratoga Oil Field.

The second marker (intersection of FM 787 and Ghost Road) is one mile north of Saratoga in the vicinity of the ghost town of Bragg. The topic, however, is not one most people would anticipate. It is for the Ghost Road and what has come to be known as the Big Thicket Light, Saratoga Light, or Bragg Light. The road follows what was previously the bed of a railroad branch line that served the McShane Lumber Company in the Dearborn settlement. As the marker text notes, "Tales of a ghostly light began even as the line was in service, before

The Texas monument is one of only a few on the Bentonville battlefield in North Carolina. *Courtesy of Texas Historical Commission.*

automobiles ran through the area." Archer Fullingim, a colorful local newspaper editor, kept the story alive through his writings, enticing a stream of regular visitors in the evenings. Their accounts of close encounters with the light, which apparently had the ability to float about the area swamps or travel at high speeds, often in pursuit of frightened onlookers, spread the legend even farther. According to the marker, "Explanations over the years have included the natural—swamp gas or reflection of phosphoric foxfire; the historical—gold hidden by Spanish soldiers and explorers; as well as the supernatural—the spirits of a rail worker searching for his lost head, a groom looking for his murdered bride, a lost hunter, disgruntled rail workers or jayhawkers." No mention, however, of the spirit of a Confederate general seeking to assuage a battlefield loss in North Carolina.

Directions to Monument
The monument is located within the Bentonville Battlefield State Historic Site in a field east of Mill Creek Church Road at Harper House Road. For detailed information, inquire at the park visitor center, 5466 Harper House Road, south of the town of Four Oaks.

Suggested Readings
Bradley, Mark L. *The Battle of Bentonville: Last Stand in the Carolinas.* Campbell, CA: Savas Publishing, 2006.

Hughes, Nathaniel Cheairs Hughes, Jr. *Bentonville: The Final Battle of Sherman and Johnson.* Chapel Hill: University of North Carolina Press, 1996.

Epilogue

The first Texas Civil War Monuments began appearing as landmarks on the cultural landscape more than a half-century ago, and since that time they have silently served to guide tourists, to promote heritage education, and to interpret complex concepts of the past. They have also reflected in their inscriptions how a group of people choose to remember the past together and how, perhaps, those values and interpretive frames of reference change along the way. Society has evolved a great deal since the early 1960s when the Civil War was but a century old and the sons and daughters of soldiers, government leaders, home front survivors, refugees, and enslaved Americans still carried with them the stories they had heard so often from those with firsthand experiences of a particularly trying time in our past. Today, 150 years after some of the conflicts remembered here played out on distant battlefields, those real-life memories have faded away, replaced by others just as relevant and worthy of a role in the process of commemoration. The United States is a far different place than it was in the 1860s, and the struggle known as the Civil War has been an integral part of that change. Elements of it are still debated, with passions, perspectives, and purposes never imagined a century and a half ago—but they are always debated under a broader perspective of unity. Whatever role the war ultimately played in that unity and openness is for other studies by other historians, but what is known for certain, and what we believe is reflected in this book, is that people still seek out the places where history happened, even if the landscape and the underlying stories of that history have changed through time.

What we endeavored to present here is a record of how people remember the past and, in a sense, how that collective memory changes over time. That process of public interpretation is part of learning from the past, and so the focus is increasingly on education. In the words of the philosopher and writer George Santayana, who was born in Spain in

1863 as the Civil War raged in the United States, "Those who cannot learn from history are doomed to repeat it." And so there are still stories to tell and still those who want to tell the stories in new ways to new generations to move the dialogue along the continuum that is history. An example of that is ongoing even as we write: an effort to place a Texas monument on the Glorieta Battlefield in New Mexico, an effort that failed to materialize for various reasons back in the 1960s. If it happens, as it appears it may, many more people will learn about an event called the Civil War and realize that it touched Texas and Texans far more deeply than they might have originally thought. And maybe that understanding will lead to new questions to pursue, and with the questions may come new answers. In the meantime, the people keep seeking out the sites from the past—and the history keeps evolving.

At the time of publication, discussions were underway to place a Texas monument near Sharpshooters Ridge, a promontory at Pigeon's Ranch that was at the center of fighting around Glorieta, New Mexico, in March 1862. *Courtesy of Alexander Collection.*

Appendix

Civil War Generals Buried in Texas

Two leading authorities on the subject of Confederate senior military officers agree there were 425 so-called *confirmed* generals serving the Confederacy during the Civil War. Both Ezra J. Warner (*Generals in Gray: Lives of the Southern Commanders*) and Bruce S. Allardyce (*More Generals in Gray*) concur that this group of officers met some or all of the somewhat complicated requirements to legitimately qualify as Confederate generals. Allardyce, however, contends there were at least 272 others who could claim to be generals, albeit with varying degrees of legitimacy. Of this group, he considered 137 to have been *probable* generals. These were senior colonels who were either given battlefield promotions by their superior officers or men whose promotion to flag rank failed to be officially recorded. Also in this grouping are men who held a general's rank in the various state armies and militias, which served the Southern cause during the war. The remaining 135 names on Allardyce's list can best be referred to as being *possible* generals. These are officers who were shown to have held the rank by less authoritative sources, in contemporaneous military communications and correspondence, or in articles appearing in newspaper and magazine articles during the war and beyond.

The following listings identify all Confederate generals buried in Texas based on information found in the works of both Warner and Allardyce, supplemented with information from *The Handbook of Texas Online* and Findagrave.com. Not included are the names of the countless senior officers who believed they should have been raised to the higher rank but were never officially promoted. Many were able to convince family and friends, however, that they were therefore the victims of a gross oversight of historical fact. In addition to the Confederates listed here, there are three Union generals buried in Texas, and their names and burial sites are included at the end of this appendix.

Confirmed Generals

Name	Burial Site	Key Battles, Campaigns, or Service
1. Bee, Hamilton P.	San Antonio, Confederate Cemetery	Red River
2. Cabell, William L.	Dallas, Greenwood Cemetery	Corinth, Iuka, Marks' Mills
3. Ector, Mathew D.	Marshall, Greenwood Cemetery	Richmond, Elkhorn Tavern, Corinth, Vicksburg, Chickamauga
4. Gano, Richard	Dallas, Oakland Cemetery	Kentucky, Arkansas, Indian Territory, Chickamauga
5. Goggin, James	Austin, Oakwood Cemetery	Cedar Creek, Sayler's Creek
6. Granbury, Hiram B.	Granbury, Granbury Cemetery	Fort Donelson, Raymond, Jackson, Chattanooga, Chickamauga, Franklin
7. Green, Thomas	Austin, Oakwood Cemetery	Glorieta, Galveston, Red River
8. Hardeman, William	Austin, State Cemetery	Glorieta, Red River
9. Harrison, James E.	Waco, First Street Cemetery	Louisiana, Red River
10. Harrison, Thomas	Waco, Oakwood Cemetery	Shiloh, Corinth, Perryville, Stones River, Chickamauga
11. Hawthorn, Alexander	Marshall, Greenwood Cemetery	Shiloh, Red River
12. Johnson, Adam Rankin	Austin, State Cemetery	Fort Donelson, Newburgh Raid, Grubb's Crossroads
13. Johnston, Albert S.	Austin, State Cemetery	Shiloh
14. Lane, Walter P.	Marshall, Marshall Cemetery	Wilson's Creek, Elkhorn Tavern, Corinth, Franklin, Mansfield
15. McCulloch, Ben	Austin, State Cemetery	Wilson's Creek, Elkhorn Tavern
16. McCulloch, Henry	Seguin, San Geronimo Cemetery	Texas Frontier, Vicksburg Campaign, Red River
17. Magruder, John Bankhead	Galveston, Episcopal Cemetery	Seven Days, Galveston
18. Maxey, Samuel Bell	Paris, Evergreen Cemetery	Port Hudson, Indian Territory
19. Moore, John	Osage, Osage Cemetery	Shiloh, Corinth, Vicksburg, Chattanooga
20. Robertson, Felix Huston	Waco, Oakwood Cemetery	Shiloh, Murfreesboro, Chickamauga, Atlanta Campaign
21. Robertson, Jerome B.	Waco, Oakwood Cemetery	Peninsular Campaign, Fredericksburg, Gettysburg, Chickamauga
22. Ross, Lawrence Sullivan	Waco, Oakwood Cemetery	Elkhorn Tavern, Corinth, Vicksburg, Nashville-Atlanta

23. Scurry, William R.	Austin, State Cemetery	Glorieta, Galveston, Red River
24. Steele, William	Austin, Oakwood Cemetery	New Mexico, Indian Territory, Red River
25. Waterhouse, Richard	Jefferson, Oakwood Cemetery	Milliken's Bend, Red River
26. Waul, Thomas N.	Fort Worth, Greenwood Cemetery	Vicksburg, Red River, Arkansas
27. Wharton, John A.	Austin, State Cemetery	Shiloh, Perryville, Stones River, Chickamauga, Red River
28. Wigfall, Louis T.	Galveston, Trinity Episcopal Cemetery	None
29. Young, William Hugh	San Antonio, Confederate Cemetery	Corinth, Perryville, Vicksburg, Stones River, Chickamauga, Kennesaw Mountain, Allatoona

Probable Generals

Name	Burial Site	Key Battles, Campaigns, or Service
1. Anderson, Charles D.	Galveston, Old Cahill Cemetery	Shiloh, Fort Gaines
2. Bagby, Arthur P., Jr.	Hallettsville, City Cemetery	Val Verde, Galveston, Red River
3. Barnes, James W.	Anderson, Barnes Cemetery	Texas State Troops
4. Baylor, John R.	Montell, Episcopal Church of the Ascension Cemetery	New Mexico
5. Benavides, Santos	Laredo, Catholic Cemetery	Laredo
6. Cumby, Robert H.	Sulphur Springs, City Cemetery	Wilson's Creek, Elkhorn Tavern
7. DeBray, Xavier B.	Austin, State Cemetery	Galveston, Red River
8. Ford, John S.	San Antonio, Confederate Cemetery	Palmito Ranch
9. Griffith, John S.	Terrell, Oakland Memorial Cemetery	Holly Springs, Elkhorn Tavern
10. Hannon, Moses W.	Oakwood, Oakwood Cemetery	Monroe's Crossroads, Chickamauga
11. Harrison, Richard	Waco, First Street Cemetery	Corinth, Vicksburg, Atlanta, Franklin
12. King, Wilburn H.	Corsicana, Oakwood Cemetery	Wilson's Creek, Mansfield
13. Lewis, Levin	Dallas, Greenwood Cemetery	Prairie Grove
14. Mabry, Hinchie P.	Jefferson	Elkhorn Tavern
15. McAdoo, John David	Brenham, Prairie Lea Cemetery	Texas State Troops
16. Pearce, Nicholas Bartlett	Whitesboro	Wilson's Creek
17. Rains, James	Seagoville, Lee Cemetery	Elkhorn Tavern, Missouri State Guard
18. Randal, Horace	Marshall, Marshall Cemetery	Mansfield, Jenkins' Ferry

19. Robertson, Elijah	Salado, Robertson Family Cemetery	Texas Frontier
20. Terrell, Alexander	Austin, State Cemetery	Red River
21. Throckmorton, James	McKinney, Pecan Grove Cemetery	Indian Territory, Elkhorn Tavern, Mississippi, Louisiana

Possible Generals

Name	Burial Site	Key Battles, Campaigns, or Service
1. Austin, William Tennant	Galveston, Lakeview Cemetery	Texas State Troops
2. Buchel, Augustus	Austin, State Cemetery	Pleasant Hill
3. Clark, Edward	Marshall, Marshall Cemetery	Pleasant Hill
4. Hamman, William Harrison	Calvert, Calvert City Cemetery	Gaines' Mill, Texas State Troops
5. McLeod, Hugh	Austin, State Cemetery	Rio Grande, Virginia
6. Nichols, Ebenezer B.	Unknown	Galveston
7. Stapp, Darwin Massey	Victoria, Evergreen Cemetery	Matagorda Bay
8. Webb, William G.	La Grange, Old City Cemetery	Texas State Troops

Confirmed Union Generals

Name	Burial Site	Key Battles, Campaigns, or Service
1. Catterson, Robert Francis	San Antonio, National Cemetery	Vicksburg, Chattanooga, Atlanta, Bentonville
2. Davis, Edmund J.	Austin, State Cemetery	Galveston, Rio Grande
3. Hamilton, Andrew Jackson	Austin, Oakwood Cemetery	New Orleans

Bibliography

Allardyce, Bruce S. *More Generals in Gray*. Baton Rouge: Louisiana State University, 1995.

Arnold, James R. *The Armies of U. S. Grant*. London: Arms and Armour Press, 1995.

Battles and Leaders of the Civil War, 4 Vols. Edison, NJ, n.d.

Boatner, Mark M. III. *The Civil War Dictionary*. New York: Vintage Books, 1991.

Borit, Gabor S. ed. *Lincoln's Generals*. New York: Oxford University Press, 1994.

Catton, Bruce. *Grant Moves South*. Boston: Little Brown and Company, 1960.

————. *Grant Takes Command*. Boston: Little, Brown and Company, 1968-1969.

————. *The Civil War*. New York: Houghton Mifflin Company, 1987.

————. *Reflections on the Civil War*. New York: Berkley Publishing Company, 1981.

Cleaves, Freeman. *Rock of Chickamauga: The Life of General George H. Thomas*. Norman: University of Oklahoma Press, 1948.

Coddington, Edwin B. *The Gettysburg Campaign: A Study in Command*. New York: Charles Scribner's Sons, 1968.

Colton, Ray C. *The Civil War in the Western Territories: Arizona, Colorado, New Mexico and Utah*. Norman: University of Oklahoma Press, 1959.

Cozzens, Peter. *This Terrible Sound: The Battle of Chickamauga*. Champaign: University of Illinois Press, 1992.

Davis, Burke. *Gray Fox: Robert E. Lee and the Civil War*. New York: The Fairfax Press, 1956.

Dowdey, Clifford, and Louis H. Manarin, eds. *The Wartime Papers of Robert E. Lee*. New York: Da Capo Press, 1961.

DuPuy, R. Ernest, and Trevor DuPuy. *The Encyclopedia of Military History: From 3500 B.C. to the Present*. New York: Harper & Row, 1966.

Faust, Patricia L., ed. *Historical Times Illustrated Encyclopedia of the Civil War*. New York: Harper & Row, 1986.

Foote, Shelby. *The Civil War: A Narrative*, 3 Vols. New York: First Vintage Press, 1986.

Frazier, Donald S. *Blood and Treasure: Confederate Empire in the Southwest*. College Station: Texas A&M University Press, 1995.

Freeman, Douglas Southall. *Lee's Lieutenants*, 3 Vols. New York: Simon & Schuster, 1995.

Fuller, J. F. C. *Grant and Lee: A Study in Personality and Generalship*. Bloomington: Indiana University Press, 1982.

————. *The Generalship of Ulysses S. Grant*. New York: Da Capo Press, 1991.

Grant, Ulysses S. *Personal Memoirs of U. S. Grant*. New York: Da Capo Press, 1982.

Griffith, Paddy. *Battle Tactics of the Civil War*. New Haven, CT: Yale University Press, 1909.

Hart, B. H. Liddell. *Sherman: Soldier, Realist, American*. New York: Da Capo Press, 1993.

Hartwell, Richard, and Philip N. Racine, eds. *The Fiery Trail: A Union Officer's Account of Sherman's Last Campaigns*. Knoxville: The University of Tennessee Press, 1986.

Heleniak, Roman J., and Lawrence Hewitt, eds. *Leadership during the Civil War*. Shippenburg, PA: White Mane Publishing Company, 1992.

Kennedy, Frances H., ed. *The Civil War Battlefield Guide*. Arlington, VA: The Conservation Fund, 1998.

Long, A. L. *Memoirs of Robert E. Lee*. Secaucus, NJ: Blue & Grey Press, 1983.

Lyman, Theodore. *With Grant & Meade from the Wilderness to Appomattox*. Lincoln: University of Nebraska Press, 1994.

McPherson, James M. *Battle Cry of Freedom: The Civil War Era*. New York: Ballantine Books, 1988.

Macdonald, John. *Great Battles of the Civil War*. New York: Macmillan, 1992.

Sears, Stephen W. *George B. McClellan: The Young Napoleon*. New York: Ticknor & Fields, 1988.

Sifakis, Stewart. *Compendium of the Confederate Armies: Texas*. Westminster, MA: Willow Bend Books, 2008.

Symonds, Craig L. A. *Battlefield Atlas of the Civil War*. Baltimore: The Nautical and Aviation Publishing Company of America, 1983.

Texas Historical Commission. Official Texas Historical Marker files. Austin, Texas.

Texas State Library. "Out of State Historical Marker Files." Austin, Texas.

Thomas, Emory M. *Robert E. Lee: A Biography*. New York: W. W. Norton & Company, 1995.

Thompson, Jerry D. *Confederate General of the West: Henry Hopkins Sibley*. College Station: Texas A&M University Press, 1996.

Utley, Robert M. *Fort Union National Monument*. Washington: National Park Service, 1962.

Vandiver, Frank E. *Rebel Brass: The Confederate Command System*. Baton Rouge: Louisiana State University Press, 1984.

Warner, Ezra J. *Generals in Blue: Lives of the Union Commanders*. Baton Rouge: Louisiana State University Press, 1992.

———. *Generals in Gray: Lives of the Confederate Commanders*. Baton Rouge: Louisiana State University Press, 1959.

Welch, Jack D. *Medical Histories of Confederate Generals*. Kent, OH: Kent State University Press, 1964.

Williams, T. Hardy. *Lincoln and His Generals*. New York: Random House, 1952.

———. *McClellan, Sherman and Grant*. New Brunswick, NJ: Rutgers University Press, 1962.

Woodworth, Steven E. *Jefferson Davis and His Generals: The Failure of Confederate Command in the West*. Lawrence: University of Kansas Press, 1990.

Wooster, Ralph A. *Texas and Texans in the Civil War*. Austin: Eakin Press, 1995.

About the Authors

Thomas E. Alexander, Vice-Chairman of the Texas Historical Commission (THC), was appointed to the THC by Governor Rick Perry in 2003. A former Air Force officer, rancher, and retired Executive Vice President of Neiman Marcus, he is a graduate of the University of Colorado and holds a master's degree from the American Military University with Honors in Civil War Studies and was named the university's Distinguished Graduate in 2012. He is the author of six other books, including the Rupert Richardson award-winning *The One and Only Rattlesnake Bomber Base* also published by State House Press.

Dan K. Utley, a native of East Texas, holds degrees in history from the University of Texas and Sam Houston State University. He retired from the Texas Historical Commission in 2007 as chief historian, and soon after he began teaching at Texas State University, where he now also serves as chief historian of the Center for Texas Public History. He is the coauthor of several books on Texas history, including *History Ahead: Stories beyond the Texas Roadside Markers* (with Cynthia J. Beeman), winner of the Award of Merit from the Philosophical Society of Texas in 2012. He is a past president of the East Texas Historical Association and the Texas Oral History Association and the former chairman of the National Register State Board of Review for Texas. A Fellow of the Texas State Historical Association, he is a recipient of the Thomas L. Charlton Award for Lifetime Achievement in Oral History.

Index

CPSIA information can be obtained at www.ICGtesting.com
Printed in the USA
LVOW13s0018280813

349795LV00003B/7/P